Anonymus

Return of judicial Rents fixed by Sub-Commissioners and Civil Bill Courts

Notified to Irish Land Commission, April 1897

Anonymus

Return of judicial Rents fixed by Sub-Commissioners and Civil Bill Courts
Notified to Irish Land Commission, April 1897

ISBN/EAN: 9783741196522

Manufactured in Europe, USA, Canada, Australia, Japa

Cover: Foto ©Lupo / pixelio.de

Manufactured and distributed by brebook publishing software
(www.brebook.com)

Anonymus

Return of judicial Rents fixed by Sub-Commissioners and Civil Bill Courts

Irish Land Commission.

Land Law Acts.

RETURN

ACCORDING TO PROVINCES AND COUNTIES

OF

JUDICIAL RENTS

FIXED BY

SUB-COMMISSIONS AND CIVIL BILL COURTS,

FOR FIRST AND SECOND STATUTORY TERMS,

TOGETHER WITH A RETURN PREPARED IN A SIMILAR MANNER OF JUDICIAL RENTS THAT HAVE BEEN REVISED BY THE LAND COMMISSION ON APPEAL, AS NOTIFIED DURING THE MONTH OF

APRIL, 1897,

ALSO

RENTS FIXED UPON THE REPORTS OF VALUERS APPOINTED BY THE IRISH LAND COMMISSION ON THE JOINT APPLICATIONS OF LANDLORDS AND TENANTS.

Presented to both Houses of Parliament by Command of Her Majesty.

DUBLIN:
PRINTED FOR HER MAJESTY'S STATIONERY OFFICE,
BY ALEXANDER THOM & CO. (LIMITED).

And to be purchased, either directly or through any Bookseller, from
HODGES, FIGGIS, and Co. (LIMITED), 104, Grafton-street, Dublin; or
EYRE and SPOTTISWOODE, East Harding-street, Fleet-street, E.C.; or
JOHN MENZIES and Co., 12, Hanover-street, Edinburgh, and 90, West Nile-street, Glasgow.

1897.

I.

RETURN

ACCORDING TO PROVINCES AND COUNTIES

OF

JUDICIAL RENTS

FIXED BY

SUB-COMMISSIONS AND CIVIL BILL COURTS,

FOR FIRST AND SECOND STATUTORY TERMS.

AS NOTIFIED DURING THE MONTH OF

APRIL, 1897,

ALSO

RENTS FIXED UPON THE REPORTS OF VALUERS APPOINTED BY THE IRISH LAND COMMISSION ON THE JOINT APPLICATIONS OF LANDLORDS AND TENANTS.

INDEX.

SUMMARIES FOR APRIL, 1897.

FIRST STATUTORY TERM.

Summary showing, according to Provinces and Counties, the Number of Cases in which Judicial Rents have been Fixed by Sub-Commissions under the Land Law (Ireland) Act, 1881, for a *First Statutory Term*, during the Month of April, 1897; and also the Acreage, Tenement Valuations, Former Rents, and Judicial Rents of the Holdings.

Province and County.	Number of Cases in which Judicial Rents have been fixed.	Acreage.	Tenement Valuation.	Former Rent.	Judicial Rent.
		Statute Measure. A. R. P.	£ s. d.	£ s. d.	£ s. d.
ULSTER—					
Antrim, ...	8	91 1 30	85 5 0	81 10 11	71 11 6
Armagh, ...	27	841 0 17	807 10 0	718 14 0	139 12 6
Cavan, ...	4	137 2 4	84 6 0	84 8 0	57 18 0
Donegal, ...	7	374 1 10	103 5 0	107 4 6	77 13 [illegible]
Down, ...	33	385 0 0	336 15 3	873 6 9	378 17 6
Fermanagh, ...	9	841 2 3	91 5 0	109 3 0	77 15 1
Londonderry, ...	1	31 0 10	14 5 0	16 2 6	11 14 1
Monaghan, ...	7	823 3 33	101 6 0	99 3 0	82 11 3
Tyrone, ...	30	865 0 36	396 5 0	379 10 8	323 13 [illegible]
Total, ...	113	2,383 0 13	1,751 19 8	1,344 11 4	915 11 1
LEINSTER—					
Carlow, ...	1	6 1 36	1 0 0	1 0 0	1 16 3
Dublin, ...	6	138 3 30	166 0 0	191 14 0	179 15 6
Kildare, ...	1	18 0 0	6 0 0	5 0 0	4 10 3
Kilkenny, ...	8	149 3 0	98 0 0	134 8 9	89 8 8
King's, ...	3	66 1 27	77 0 0	77 0 0	75 11 8
Louth, ...	38	377 8 8	393 15 0	870 14 3	305 1 4
Meath, ...	6	187 2 18	190 0 0	139 15 1	137 13 9
Queen's, ...	4	174 0 4	61 0 0	80 2 6	77 11 5
Wexford, ...	35	1,489 2 31	760 0 0	743 2 10	537 0 11
Total, ...	91	2,891 2 31	1,461 15 0	1,685 16 1	1,237 4 11
CONNAUGHT—					
Mayo, ...	4	149 2 17	75 0 0	128 6 1	93 5 0
MUNSTER—					
Clare, ...	3	180 1 5	100 5 0	180 0 0	86 8 1
Cork, ...	8	226 1 7	157 15 0	192 0 8	164 1 1
Tipperary, ...	7	19 2 8	21 0 0	25 0 0	15 5 7
Total, ...	18	426 0 16	278 19 0	347 0 8	261 15 4

IRELAND.

ULSTER, ...	113	2,383 0 13	1,751 19 8	1,344 11 4	915 11 1
LEINSTER, ...	91	2,891 2 31	1,461 15 0	1,635 18 4	1,237 4 11
CONNAUGHT, ...	4	149 2 17	75 0 0	128 6 1	93 6 0
MUNSTER, ...	18	426 0 16	278 19 0	347 0 5	261 15 4
TOTALS, ...	226	5,850 1 38	3,567 18 8	3,343 16 5	2,469 16 7

CIVIL BILL COURTS.

SUMMARY FOR APRIL, 1897.

FIRST STATUTORY TERM.

Cases in which Judicial Rents have been Fixed by Civil Bill Courts, under the Land Law (Ireland) Act, 1881, for a *First Statutory Term*, and notified to the Irish Land Commission during the Month of April, 1897.

Province and County.	Number of Cases in which Judicial Rents have been fixed.	Acreage.	Poor Law Valuation.	Former Rent.	Judicial Rent.
		Statute Measure. A. R. P.	£ s. d.	£ s. d.	£ s. d.
ULSTER—					
Cavan, ...	3	39 3 35	30 10 0	23 19 11	16 5 0
LEINSTER—					
Kilkenny, ...	20	611 1 9	700 10 0	771 5 8	601 1 0
Louth, ...	9	316 0 13	94 10 0	90 0 3	79 14 5
Queen's, ...	4	113 3 38	79 5 0	65 6 6	61 10 6
Wicklow, ...	1	5 3 20	-	6 1 8	5 11 0
Total, ...	34	1,079 3 0	883 5 0	933 10 7	704 3 5
MUNSTER—					
Cork, ...	8	248 1 29	138 5 0	150 8 0	117 1 6
Kerry, ...	9	537 0 11½	64 16 0	136 12 8	90 0 0
Limerick, ...	1	19 1 5	53 0 0	87 0 0	20 0 0
Total, ...	18	804 3 5½	256 0 0	374 0 8	231 1 6

IRELAND.

Province.	Number of Cases	Acreage	Poor Law Valuation	Former Rent	Judicial Rent
ULSTER, ...	3	39 2 35	30 10 0	23 12 11	16 5 0
LEINSTER, ...	34	1,079 0 0	883 5 0	955 10 7	704 3 5
MUNSTER, ...	18	804 3 5½	268 0 0	374 0 8	231 1 6
TOTALS, ...	55	1,914 1 0½	1,183 15 0	1,378 4 0	951 8 11

LEASEHOLDERS.

FIRST STATUTORY TERM.

SUMMARY FOR APRIL, 1897.

Summary showing, according to Provinces and Counties, the Number of Cases in which Judicial Rents have been Fixed by Chief Commission and Sub-Commissions, under the Land Law (Ireland) Act, 1887, and the Redemption of Rent (Ireland) Act, 1891, for a *First Statutory Term*, during the Month of April, 1897; and also the Acreages, Tenement Valuations, Former Rents, and Judicial Rents of the Holdings.

Province and County.		Number of Cases in which Judicial Rents have been fixed.	Acreage.	Tenement Valuation.	Former Rent.	Judicial Rent.
			Statute Measure.			
			A. R. P.	£ s. d.	£ s. d.	£ s. d.
ULSTER—						
Antrim,	...	1	22 3 18	40 0 0	18 18 6	19 0 0
Cavan,	...	1	33 1 [illegible]	33 0 0	[illegible] 0 0	18 15 0
Down,	...	1	66 1 7	45 0 0	45 0 0	36 0 0
Tyrone,	...	8	[illegible] 0 6	158 16 0	157 16 8	197 16 6
Total,	...	11	348 3 13	232 16 0	248 14 11	191 11 6
LEINSTER—						
Dublin,	...	1	31 0 19	75 0 0	91 8 2	[illegible] 0 0
King's,	...	1	36 0 19	—	87 10 0	[illegible] 0 0
Queen's,	...	4	430 1 0	200 8 0	280 8 7	273 14 6
Wexford,	...	1	167 0 35	152 0 0	141 8 4	97 0 0
Total,	...	7	728 1 15	427 8 0	536 8 10	488 14 6
MUNSTER—						
Clare,	...	1	40 0 35	30 10 0	81 3 6	41 17 6
Cork,	...	5	451 1 14	327 5 0	479 0 6	318 8 6
Tipperary,	...	1	13 0 [illegible]	18 0 0	32 11 [illegible]	16 0 0
Total,	...	9	504 2 35	373 15 0	493 17 1	403 14 6

IRELAND.

ULSTER,	...	11	348 3 13	232 16 0	248 14 11	191 11 6
LEINSTER,	...	7	728 1 15	427 8 0	536 8 10	488 14 6
MUNSTER,	...	9	504 2 35	373 15 0	493 17 1	403 14 6
TOTALS,	...	27	1,582 3 23	1,033 16 0	1,277 0 10	1,083 0 6

CIVIL BILL COURTS.

LEASEHOLDERS.

FIRST STATUTORY TERM.

SUMMARY FOR APRIL, 1897.

Cases in which Judicial Rents have been Fixed by Civil Bill Courts under the Land Law (Ireland) Act, 1887, for a *First Statutory Term*, and notified to the Irish Land Commission, during the Month of April, 1897.

Province and County.	Number of Cases in which Judicial Rents have been fixed.	Acreage.	Tenement Valuation.	Former Rent.	Judicial Rent.
		Statute Measure.			
LEINSTER—		A. R. P.	£ s. d.	£ s. d.	£ s. d.
Kilkenny, ...	2	71 0 35	61 5 0	68 0 0	57 0 0
Louth, ...	1	78 3 7	83 10 0	117 4 0	85 7 4
Queen's, ...	1	74 2 1	30 0 0	50 0 0	36 0 0
Total, ...	4	224 2 3	174 15 0	235 4 0	178 7 4

IRELAND.

SUMMARIES FOR APRIL, 1897.

SECOND STATUTORY TERM.

Summary showing, according to Provinces and Counties, the Number of Cases in which Judicial Rents have been Fixed by Sub-Commissions under the Land Law (Ireland) Act, 1881, for a *Second Statutory Term*, during the Month of April, 1897; and also the Acreage, Tenement Valuations, Rents of the Holdings prior to the creation of First Statutory Term, Judicial Rents for First Statutory Term, and the Judicial Rents for a Second Statutory Term.

Province and County		Number of Cases in which Judicial Rents have been fixed	Acreage. Statute Measure. A.	R.	P.	Tenement Valuation. £	s.	d.	Rent of Holdings prior to creation of First Statutory Term. £	s.	d.	Judicial Rent for First Statutory Term. £	s.	d.	Judicial Rent for a Second Statutory Term. £	s.	d.
ULSTER—																	
Antrim,	...	40	1,098	1	38	625	5	0	1,071	14	6	831	19	10	510	1	6
Armagh,	...	94	1,376	1	26	1,398	10	6	1,600	17	5½	1,187	0	10	606	4	4
Cavan,	...	36	948	0	9	692	6	6	813	11	8½	660	1	5	513	13	9
Donegal,	...	35	1,047	3	18	460	19	0	578	1	11	453	17	11	345	19	6
Down,	...	84	2,084	3	17	2,213	5	9	2,301	4	1	1,938	14	4	1,380	19	4
Fermanagh,	...	36	383	1	24	732	15	0	394	13	6	763	15	0	187	0	6
Londonderry,	...	87	780	3	14	403	5	6	504	12	8½	388	17	0	337	15	6
Monaghan,	...	27	668	2	37	845	0	0	165	10	[illegible]	360	8	11	280	16	5
Tyrone,	...	145	3,898	0	38	2,076	13	10	3,373	3	8½	2,111	7	3	1,631	9	4
Total,	...	501	11,934	8	1	8,579	17	10	10,440	14	10	8,163	13	11	6,968	9	1
LEINSTER—																	
Dublin,	...	4	100	0	31	67	5	0	144	0	0	131	6	0	98	15	9
King's,	...	5	136	1	33	88	5	0	193	11	0	96	1	0	80	0	6
Louth,	...	16	157	1	34	96	4	0	167	11	6	107	10	0	86	12	6
Meath,	...	4	370	1	35	253	15	0	357	13	0	368	15	6	260	10	6
Queen's,	...	17	1,079	0	4	616	6	0	1,343	9	1	620	4	0	713	14	6
Wexford,	...	4	523	1	16	336	15	0	353	10	4	895	0	0	197	0	6
Total,	...	49	2,368	3	25	1,437	13	0	2,557	14	9	1,854	16	4	1,475	14	9
MUNSTER—																	
Clare,	...	13	563	0	5	304	17	0	409	7	8	286	13	0	238	9	9
Cork,	...	16	944	8	10	534	6	0	973	15	8	784	0	0	615	5	9
Total,	...	30	1,413	2	36	839	2	0	1,383	3	2	1,073	13	0	853	17	0

IRELAND.

			A.	R.	P.	£	s.	d.	£	s.	d.	£	s.	d.	£	s.	d.
ULSTER,	...	501	11,934	6	1	8,579	17	10	10,440	14	10	8,163	13	11	6,969	8	1
LEINSTER,	...	49	2,368	8	25	1,437	13	0	2,557	14	9	1,854	16	4	1,475	14	9
MUNSTER,	...	30	1,413	2	36	839	2	0	1,383	3	2	1,073	13	0	853	17	0
Total,	...	580	15,606	1	12	10,856	13	10	14,180	12	9	11,110	1	8	8,287	16	1

CIVIL BILL COURTS.

SECOND STATUTORY TERM.

SUMMARY FOR APRIL, 1897.

Cases in which Judicial Rents have been fixed by Civil Bill Courts, under the Land Law (Ireland) Act, 1881, *for a Second Statutory Term*, and notified to the Irish Land Commission during the Month of April, 1897.

Province and County.		Number of Cases in which Judicial Rents have been fixed.	Acreage.	Tenement Valuation.	Rent of Holdings Prior to Commencement of First Statutory Term.	Judicial Rent for First Statutory Term.	Judicial Rent for a Second Statutory Term.
			Statute Measure.				
			A. R. P.	£ s. d.	£ s. d.	£ s. d.	£ s. d.
LEINSTER—							
Kilkenny,	...	7	310 1 15	179 10 0	205 1 2	150 3 8	116 10 0
Louth,	...	4	176 0 26	168 5 0	291 9 8	224 0 0	178 12 1
Total,	...	11	486 2 1	347 15 0	496 10 10	374 3 6	295 2 1
MUNSTER—							
Cork,	...	8	397 0 38	196 5 0	321 8 8	272 0 0	187 10 0
Kerry,	...	1	91 0 20	26 10 0	37 19 4	35 0 0	34 0 0
Limerick,	...	11	83 3 37	134 10 0	200 9 3	150 4 0	131 17 0
Waterford,	...	1	0 3 9	9 0 0	4 10 0	3 10 0	8 0 0
Total,	...	21	579 3 34	361 5 0	575 8 3	465 14 0	325 7 0

IRELAND.

LEINSTER,	...	11	486 2 1	317 15 0	496 10 10	374 8 6	295 2 1
MUNSTER,	...	21	579 3 34	361 5 0	575 8 8	465 14 0	325 7 0
TOTALS,	...	32	1,066 0 35	669 0 0	1,071 19 1	839 17 6	620 9 1

PROVINCE OF

COUNTY OF

Names of Assistant Commissioners by whom Cases were heard.	Record Number.	Date of Order.	Name of Tenant.	Name of Landlord.	Poor Law Union.	Townland.
Assistant Commissioners—		1897.				
W. F. Bailey (Legal). W. H. G. Eyre. J. Armstrong.	[illegible]	Apr. 14,	Elizabeth Taggart Executrix of Jas. Taggart, deceased.	Mrs. E. J. Baird, ...	Antrim, ...	[illegible] ...
D. Toomey (Legal). Thos. Davidson. C. H. Bolster.	8580	,,	George Woods, ...	Count Ugo Balzani, ...	Larne, ...	[illegible] ...
	8585	,,	Jane Gillespie, ...	Isabella Woods, ...	do. ...	[illegible] ...
	8578	,,	David Mawhinney,	John R. Gilmore, ...	do. ...	Ballygowan, ...
	8563	,,	Samuel Forsythe, ...	P. Paget, Official Assignee of Marquis of Donegal.	do. ...	Mullaghboy.
	8562	,,	Do. ...	do.	do. ...	do. ...
	8566	,,	Randal M'Keown,	Harold W. S. Gray, ...	Ballymena,	Brae, ...
	8564	,,	Samuel Forsythe,	P. Paget, Official Assignee of the Marquis of Donegal, a bankrupt.	Larne, ...	Mullaghboy, [illegible] ...

COUNTY OF

Names of Assistant Commissioners by whom Cases were heard.	Record Number.	Date of Order.	Name of Tenant.	Name of Landlord.	Poor Law Union.	Townland.
Assistant Commissioners—	11041	Apr. 1,	Thomas Stokes, ...	Miss J. E. M. Molyneux,	Armagh, ...	[illegible] ...
J. H. Ennis (Legal). J. H. M'Connell. A. E. Swan.	11081	,,	David Thompson & another.	Countess of Charlemont,	do. ...	[illegible] ...
	11087	,,	Thomas R. Gribbin,	do.	do. ...	Ballybrannan,
W. F. Bailey (Legal). W. Williams. G. M. Harvey.	11162	Apr. 14,	Patrick Hart, ...	T. M. H. Chambre, ...	Kerry, ...	Adrivale, ...
	11152	,,	Anne Teal, ...	In Chancery. Mark S. Synnott, a lunatic.	do. ...	[illegible] ...
	11170	,,	Patrick Gallagher,	do.	do. ...	[illegible] ...
	11230	,,	James Patterson, ...	do.	do. ...	Lurgan, ...
	11017	,,	Susan Hawthorne,	do. ...	do. ...	[illegible] & Ballinteggart
	11018	,,	James Conn, ...	do.	do. ...	Ballinteggart

ULSTER.

ANTRIM.

Extent of Holding. Statute.	Poor Law Valuation.	Present Rent.	Judicial Rent.	Observations.	Value of Tenancy.
A. R. P.	£ s. d.	£ s. d.	£ s. d.		£ s. d.
22 3 6	7 10 0	14 1 4	5 5 0		
20 1 25	16 10 0	11 13 11	9 7 6		
3 1 30	unascertained.	3 0 0	1 8 0		
9 1 25	5 10 0	5 14 0	5 7 6		
4 0 7	7 5 0	5 15 8	4 5 0		
7 0 14	unascertained.	9 3 4	4 13 5		
3 0 31	1 10 0	2 0 0	1 6 0		
15 0 0	unascertained.	20 1 8	7 10 0		
91 1 30	33 5 0	61 16 11	37 11 4		

ARMAGH.

Extent of Holding. Statute.	Poor Law Valuation.	Present Rent.	Judicial Rent.	Observations.	Value of Tenancy.
19 3 4	13 15 0	16 4 2	8 12 0		
7 1 20	9 15 0	6 12 0	5 13 0		
8 2 30	9 5 0	5 0 3	5 5 0		
5 0 0	unascertained.	6 1 10	2 15 0		
6 3 13	4 0 0	3 5 6	9 8 0		
8 3 20	3 15 0	3 17 8	3 15 0		
21 1 35	26 10 0	16 5 0	14 13 0		
20 3 20	14 10 6	9 15 0	7 10 0		

FIRST STATUTORY TERM.

COUNTY OF

Names of Assistant Commissioners by whom Cases were decided.	Record Number.	Date of Order.	Name of Tenant.	Name of Landlord.	Poor Law Union.	Townland.
Assistant Commissioners—		1897.				
	11316	Apr. 14,	William Hyde, ...	In Chancery. Mark S. Synnott, a lunatic.	Newry, ...	Ballintemple,
W. F. Bailey (Legal).	11104	"	David Graham, ...	do.	do. ...	do. ...
W. Williams.	11103	"	William Martin, ...	do. ...	do. ...	do. ...
G. Harvey.	11122	"	Terence Hand, ...	do. ...	do. ...	Aughanunshin,
	11102	"	Terence M'Keown & another,	do.	do. ...	do. ...
	11160	"	Andrew Biddle, ...	do.	do. ...	do. ...
	11120	"	Do. ...	do.	do. ...	do. ...
	11031	"	Hugh S. Patterson,	do. ...	do. ...	Lurgan, ...
	11110	"	William Gordon and another,	Maxwell C. Close, ...	do. ...	Cavan, ...
	11109	"	Do. ...	do.	do. ...	Lisnish, ...
	11108	"	William Gordon,	do.	do. ...	do. ...
	11097	"	John Lynch, ...	do.	do. ...	[illegible], ...
	11310	"	James Neal, ...	Jas. Wilson, ...	do. ...	Lisnalee, ...
						Total, ...

COUNTY OF

Names of Assistant Commissioners by whom Cases were decided.	Record Number.	Date of Order.	Name of Tenant.	Name of Landlord.	Poor Law Union.	Townland.
Assistant Commissioners—	7443	Apr. 7,	Mary Anne Johnston,	Major H. K. Maxwell,	Cavan, ...	Lisdaff, ...
	7491	"	Peter Tully, ...	Earl of Lanesborough,	do. ...	Drumbeyhan.
J. H. Edge (Legal).	7464	"	Rose Boylan, ...	Robert Story, ...	do. ...	Cavan, ...
J. O'Callaghan.	7448	"	Michael Reilly, ...	do.	do. ...	do. ...
L. Cassidy.	7170	"	Pras. M'Nerney, ...	do.	do. ...	do. ...
	7469	"	Alex. Tweedie, Ld. Admr. of John Tweedie, deceased.	Wm. Humphreys, ...	do. ...	Drumaloghe & Ballyrusky.
						Total, ...

COUNTY OF

FIRST STATUTORY TERM.

ARMAGH—*continued.*

Extent of Holding. Statute.	Poor Law Valuation.	Former Rent.	Judicial Rent.	Observations.	Value of Tenancy.
A. R. P.	£ s. d.	£ s. d.	£ s. d.		£ s. d.
13 3 35	13 15 0	8 1 8	5 15 0		
15 3 34	unascertained.	6 10 0	4 10 0		
16 3 7	do.	6 10 0	4 4 0		
6 0 25	3 10 0	5 5 0	2 14 0		
9 1 33	5 10 0	4 15 0	2 15 0		
7 0 6	1 0 0	3 0 4	2 15 0		
16 1 20	5 15 0	5 10 6	3 18 0		
39 3 0	unascertained.	30 3 7	23 0 0		
11 3 10	13 5 0	11 10 0	7 14 0		
70 3 4	25 5 0	18 0 0	15 8 0		
34 0 34	33 10 0	30 0 0	21 10 0		
7 3 24	4 10 0	5 19 4	5 15 0		
6 1 17	4 0 0	4 0 0	4 0 0		
341 0 17	209 10 0	218 14 0	148 13 0		

CAVAN.

Extent of Holding. Statute.	Poor Law Valuation.	Former Rent.	Judicial Rent.	Observations.	Value of Tenancy.
13 0 8	9 16 0	12 10 8	9 10 0		
17 3 35	17 6 0	13 13 4	10 10 0		
24 1 78	15 1 0	13 0 0	10 15 0		
33 0 11	14 10 0	16 4 0	13 5 0		
10 0 17	6 5 0	7 0 0	5 5 0		
39 0 0	21 10 0	25 0 0	20 10 0		
137 3 4	84 8 0	88 8 0	67 16 0		

DONEGAL.

Extent of Holding. Statute.	Poor Law Valuation.	Former Rent.	Judicial Rent.	Observations.	Value of Tenancy.
56 3 30	45 0 0	63 18 0	35 0 0		
10 2 15	4 10 0	9 14 6	4 14 2		
11 1 6	7 10 0	7 13 0	5 13 1		
4 1 30	4 10 0	5 7 0	4 10 3		

COUNTY OF

Names of Assistant Commissioners by whom Court was divided.	Record Number.	Date of Order.	Name of Tenant.	Name of Landlord.	Poor Law Union.	Townland.
Assistant Commissioners—		1887.				
G. H. Tebbing (Legal). R. H. Pringle. J. A. Smith.	13707	Apr. 19,	John Donaldson, ..	Solomon H. Darcus and ors.	Stranorlar,	Ballinamore, ..
	13578	"	Owen M'Gilloway,	R. N. Chatterton & anor., Trustees of William Young, deceased,	do. ...	Corvalley, ..
	13456	"	James Stewart, ...	H. G. Murray Stewart,	Glenties, ...	Crossroagh,
						Total, ..

COUNTY OF

Names of Assistant Commissioners by whom Court was divided.	Record Number.	Date of Order.	Name of Tenant.	Name of Landlord.	Poor Law Union.	Townland.
Assistant Commissioners— W. F. Bailey (Legal). S. Byers. S. G. Williams.	12287	Apr. 14,	Roger Walsh, ...	Alexander H. Gordon,	Newtownards	Drumreagh, ..
	17326	"	John Brown,	do.	do. ...	Ballyboonie,
	18100	"	William Baxter, ...	David Dalzell, ...	do. ...	Tullyvaill, ..
	18101	"	Do., ...	do.	do. ...	Ringneal, ..
	12854	"	William Burrows,	Captain Richard W. B. Ker,	do. ...	Ferrans, ..
	17083	"	William Magowan,	do.	do. ...	Ballyisbelly,
	12375	"	Mary Quinn, ...	Marquis of Dufferin and Ava,	do. ...	Ballyrolley Major,
	12868	"	Barbara Adair, ...	Robert P. Maxwell, ...	do. ...	Ouseda, ..
W. F. Bailey (Legal). A. Boxhall. W. Small.	12267	Apr. 14,	Thomas Dawson, ...	A. H. Ruddell, ...	Lurgan, ...	Ballydugan,
	12264	"	Robert Dawson, ...	do.	do. ...	do. ..
	12258	"	Thomas Adamson,	do.	do. ...	do. ..
	12497	"	Robert Wilson, ...	do.	do. ...	do. ..
	12281	"	Thomas Dawson, ...	do.	do. ...	do. ..
	12269	"	Bernard O'Neill, ...	do.	do. ...	do. ..
	12348	"	Do., ...	do.	do. ...	do. ..
	12345	"	James Topping, senior,	do.	do. ...	do. ..
	17284	"	Timothy Kennedy,	do.	do. ...	do. ..
	18343	"	Andrew Watson, ...	do.	do. ...	do. ..
	12263	"	Margaret [illegible] & others,	do.	do. ...	do. ..
	12261	"	James M'Corville,	do.	do. ...	do. ..
	18040	"	Edward Sturgeon,	do.	do. ...	do. ..
	18259	"	Sarah Bryan, ...	do.	do. ...	do. ..
						Total, ..

DONEGAL—*continued.*

[illegible]	[illegible]	[illegible]	[illegible]	[illegible]	[illegible]
a. r. p.	£ s. d.	£ s. d.	£ s. d.		£ s. d.
61 1 10	27 0 0	24 0 0	18 15 0		
[illegible] 0 0	7 15 0	8 0 0	6 0 0		
87 0 0	1 0 0	6 14 0	1 10 0		
876 3 10	365 0 0	107 4 6	77 15 7		

DOWN.

30 0 7	33 0 0	31 3 10	15 0 0		
0 0 [illegible]	—	1 1 0	0 12 0		
30 1 15	17 5 0	17 0 0	10 15 0		
24 3 0	27 0 0	15 15 0	10 16 0		
14 1 24	15 0 0	15 0 0	9 10 0		
31 2 16	13 0 0	18 19 0	16 0 0		
[illegible] 1 [illegible]	43 0 0	[illegible] 0 0	35 0 0		
[illegible] 0 [illegible]	75 10 0	45 0 0	30 0 0		
3 0 20	8 10 0	3 8 0	1 8 0		
1 1 10	8 10 0	1 6 6	0 16 6		
32 0 0	[illegible] 10 0	30 1 0	23 18 0		
8 0 [illegible]	5 0 0	6 7 10	1 18 0		
8 1 6	3 10 0	8 13 0	3 10 0		
[illegible] 3 10	65 15 0	[illegible] 11 10	21 15 0		
4 0 0	6 15 0	5 13 6	3 0 4		
3 1 0	8 15 0	6 10 7	4 4 8		
5 0 [illegible]	6 0 0	5 [illegible] 0	7 10 0		
0 3 10	6 0 0	[illegible] 10 0	3 0 6		
1 1 0	3 5 0	1 16 0	1 0 0		
1 0 0	1 10 0	1 13 6	1 2 6		
1 3 0	5 0 0	1 16 0	1 5 0		
7 0 0	5 0 0	6 9 8	1 17 0		
[illegible] 0 0	[illegible] 13 0	877 4 9	[illegible] 17 0		

FIRST STATUTORY TERM.

COUNTY OF

Names of Assistant Commissioners by whom Cases were decided.	Record Number.	Date of Order.	Name of Tenant.	Name of Landlord.	Poor Law Union.	Townland.
Assistant Commissioners—		1887.				
A. B. Deane. R. J. Craig.	5778	Mar. 23,	Samuel Crawford, ...	Constantine Maguire, a lunatic, by E. M. Maguire, his Committee,	Enniskillen,	Tullanaig, ...
J. H. Keon (Legal). G. A. O. Adamson. W. Jeffcott.	5789	Apr. 6,	Anne Johnston, ...	Earl of Erne, ...	Clones, ...	Clevagh, ...
	5776	"	John Keenan, ...	Lord Lanesborough, ...	do. ...	Cavanagh, ...
	5782	"	James West, ...	do.	do. ...	Clonnely, ...
	5722	"	James Warnock, ...	Lord Rathdonnell, ...	do. ...	Clonfad, ...
	5723	"	Do., ...	do.	do. ...	Clonmacate, ...
	5741	"	James M'Caffrey, ...	Miss F. C. Armstrong, ...	do. ...	Killyd, ...
	5775	"	Robert Irvine, ...	Thomas Dickson & ors.,	do. ...	Annymarran & others.
J. H. Thrasher. H. Johnston. G. M'Elderry.	5765	Apr. 22,	Anne Douglas, ...	Rev. Edward Denny, ...	Lisnaskea, ...	Aghlaney, ...
						Total, ...

COUNTY OF

Names of Assistant Commissioners by whom Cases were decided.	Record Number.	Date of Order.	Name of Tenant.	Name of Landlord.	Poor Law Union.	Townland.
Assistant Commissioners—	6365	Mar. 31,	James M'Ewen, ...	Catherine H. Lyndsay, ...	Coleraine, ...	Ballyclough, ...
D. Tighe (Legal). L. W. Stuart. Gerald FitzGerald.	6357	"	John M'Crory, ...	Miss S. M. Torrens and another.	do. ...	Belaugh, ...
						Total, ...

COUNTY OF

Names of Assistant Commissioners by whom Cases were decided.	Record Number.	Date of Order.	Name of Tenant.	Name of Landlord.	Poor Law Union.	Townland.
Assistant Commissioners—	6378	Apr. 6,	Anne Tierney, ...	Stephen Murphy, ...	Monaghan,	Kerdeen, ...
J. H. Keon (Legal). W. Jeffcott.						
J. H. Keon. G. A. O. Adamson. W. Jeffcott.	[illegible]	Apr. 6,	Francis Brady, ...	George E. Moore, ...	Clones, ...	Corrangunta and another.
	6311	"	Robert Falls, ...	James J. M'Clelland, ...	Monaghan,	Shanroe Lough,
	6312	"	William Brennigan,	do.	do. ...	do. ...
	6313	"	James Falls, ...	do.	do. ...	do. ...
	6310	"	William Swanton, ...	do.	do. ...	do. ...
C. H. Thrasher. H. Johnston. G. M'Elderry.	6221	Feb. 22,	Pool (Bryan) M'Kenna,	Lieut.-Gen. M. Moore, ...	Clogher, ...	Creagh ...
						Total, ...

FIRST STATUTORY TERM.

FERMANAGH.

Extent of Holding. Statute.	Poor Law Valuation.	Former Rent.	Judicial Rent.	Observations.	Value of Tenancy.
A. R. P.	£ s. d.	£ s. d.	£ s. d.		£ s. d.
6 0 34	5 10 0	6 0 0	4 6 0		
194 1 19	unascertained,	85 0 0	60 0 0		
10 3 25	5 8 0	6 0 0	4 7 0		
15 1 18	19 10 0	14 7 8	11 15 0		
11 1 0	10 0 0	10 0 0	8 12 0		
7 0 5	5 6 0	5 0 0	4 0 0		
6 3 15	6 18 0	5 11 4	3 13 6		
36 3 0	28 16 0	18 0 0	15 5 0		
11 0 7	8 5 0	9 0 0	6 0 0		
344 2 3	91 5 0	109 3 0	77 16 0		

LONDONDERRY.

Extent of Holding. Statute.	Poor Law Valuation.	Former Rent.	Judicial Rent.	Observations.	Value of Tenancy.
16 0 0	12 0 0	13 2 6	10 16 6		
5 0 10	4 5 0	5 0 0	3 18 0		
21 0 10	16 5 0	18 2 6	14 14 6		

MONAGHAN.

Extent of Holding. Statute.	Poor Law Valuation.	Former Rent.	Judicial Rent.	Observations.	Value of Tenancy.
73 0 18	14 6 0	14 13 0	9 0 0	By consent.	
19 0 18	19 10 0	18 0 0	12 5 0		
19 2 19	13 0 0	16 0 0	9 10 0		
30 0 30	13 10 0	18 0 0	11 0 0		
5 0 16	5 10 0	6 0 0	3 10 0		
9 1 20	6 18 0	7 0 0	6 3 0		
178 1 37	23 15 0	19 0 0	14 0 0		
723 [illegible] 23	101 5 0	98 3 0	68 18 0		

...am Kelly, ...	do.
...n Dunaghey, ...	do.
...ard Kelly, ...	do.
...rew Irwin, ...	James
Do., ...	do.
... Loughran, Ltd.	do.

TYRONE.

Extent of Holding. Statute.	Poor Law Valuation.	Present Rent.	Judicial Rent.	Observations.	Value of Tenancy.
A. R. P.	£ s. d.	£ s. d.	£ s. d.		£ s. d.
3 3 10	8 18 0	4 5 0	3 18 4		
11 3 17	7 5 0	7 0 0	5 5 0		
18 0 13	8 15 0	8 8 0	6 3 0		
22 3 9	7 10 0	10 6 3	7 0 0		
3 3 30	2 10 0	4 4 0	3 1 8		
6 1 16	8 0 0	7 7 0	4 11 6		
6 1 22	8 0 0	6 0 0	3 16 8		
8 3 11	5 0 0	6 10 0	6 5 6		
10 0 37	8 0 0	9 4 8	8 18 0		
7 1 39	6 0 0	4 5 10	4 8 8		
17 1 10	15 0 0	16 15 0	11 18 0		
44 1 30	18 0 0	19 5 0	18 0 0		
7 2 8	3 8 0	1 12 11	1 5 0	With right of grazing 1/6th of 20 acres of other part of lands of Carra[illegible].	
13 3 18	4 12 0	3 5 10	3 13 0	do.	
13 2 0	6 8 0	6 18 0	5 0 0	By consent.	
11 2 30	6 0 0	7 3 0	5 14 0		
47 2 8	30 5 0	30 0 0	28 8 0		
15 1 29	7 10 0	7 10 0	5 4 0		
13 3 6	8 0 0	8 4 0	3 14 6		
48 1 8	5 15 0	6 15 0	5 0 0		
30 0 30	14 15 0	14 3 3	11 11 0		
11 0 16	3 15 0	6 0 0	8 10 0		
24 0 13	18 0 0	14 0 0	10 4 0		
13 3 35	15 0 0	19 10 0	4 6 0		
3 3 21	0 10 0	1 8 0	0 17 8		

COUNTY OF

Names of Assistant Commissioners by whom Cases were decided.	Record Number	Date of Order	Name of Tenant.	Name of Landlord.	Poor Law Union.	Townland.
Assistant Commissioners—		1897.				
J. H. Edge (Legal). J. Hewlett. W. Shaw.	12945	Mar. 31,	Samuel J. Cheldon,	Earl of Caledon, ...	Dungannon,	Killybrough, ...
	12917	„	Robert H. Dickson,	do.	do. ...	Killearn, ...
	12939	„	Archer O'Donnell,	Robert Shiel and anor.,	do. ...	Aughnar, ...
	12925	„	James H. Allen, ...	Viscount Charlemont, ...	do. ...	Derryhaw, ...
	12911	„	Patrick Kelly, ...	James A. King & anor.,	do. ...	Greenlady, ...
						Total, ...

PROVINCE OF

COUNTY OF

Names of Assistant Commissioners by whom Cases were decided.	Record Number	Date of Order	Name of Tenant.	Name of Landlord.	Poor Law Union.	Townland.
Assistant Commissioners— M. T. Cregan (Legal). T. A. Dillon. J. A. O'Keeffe.	2379	April 26,	Anne Mahoney, ...	The Earl of Courtown,	New Ross, ...	Lisdown, ...

COUNTY OF

Names of Assistant Commissioners by whom Cases were decided.	Record Number	Date of Order	Name of Tenant.	Name of Landlord.	Poor Law Union.	Townland.
Assistant Commissioners—	1675	April 28,	Patrick Coffe, ...	Colonel J. F. Forster, ...	Baltinglass,	Milltown and [illegible] and another.
L. Doyle (Legal). A. M. Craig. G. S. Bolster.	1677	„	Do., ...	do.	do. ...	Sextown, ...
	1676	„	Do., ...	do.	do. ...	Crossmouth, ...
	1651	„	Richard Hagan, ...	Colonel G. C. Synge, ...	do. ...	Regles, ...
	1635	„	John Brennan, ...	G. W. Langtry, ...	do. ...	Oldtown, ...
	1636	„	Michael Dennis, ...	James Cartland, ...	do. ...	Rampton, ...
						Total, ...

COUNTY OF

Names of Assistant Commissioners by whom Cases were decided.	Record Number	Date of Order	Name of Tenant.	Name of Landlord.	Poor Law Union.	Townland.
Assistant Commissioners— M. T. Cregan (Legal). J. D. Boyd. J. Germaine.	6977	Mar. 23,	Henry Burke, ...	George C. Wilson, ...	Edenderry,	Drehid, ...

FIRST STATUTORY TERM.

TYRONE—*continued.*

Extent of Holding (Statute).	Poor Law Valuation.	Former Rent.	Judicial Rent.	Observations.	Value of Tenancy.
A. R. P.	£ s. d.	£ s. d.	£ s. d.		£ s. d.
[illegible] 1 0	51 0 0	15 11 0	13 14 0		
10 [illegible] [illegible]	unascertained.	10 [illegible] 3	9 17 [illegible]		
13 [illegible] [illegible]	13 0 0	9 10 6	9 1 6		
[illegible] 0 0	21 10 0	15 0 8	10 1[illegible] 0		
13 [illegible] 9	8 10 0	7 0 0	8 7 0		
[illegible] 0 [illegible]	[illegible] 5 0	172 18 8	209 13 7		

LEINSTER.

CARLOW.

Extent of Holding (Statute).	Poor Law Valuation.	Former Rent.	Judicial Rent.	Observations.	Value of Tenancy.
6 1 36	6 0 0	6 0 0	1 15 0		

DUBLIN.

Extent of Holding (Statute).	Poor Law Valuation.	Former Rent.	Judicial Rent.	Observations.	Value of Tenancy.
8 0 38	6 10 0	8 10 0	8 10 0		
8 0 22	11 18 0	18 0 0	12 10 0		
[illegible] [illegible] 25	[illegible] 0 0	107 6 0	[illegible] 0 0		
30 1 31	14 0 0	16 0 0	13 0 0		
[illegible] 3 [illegible]	35 18 0	60 0 0	33 0 0		
6 2 16	8 0 0	9 0 0	7 18 0		
[illegible] [illegible] [illegible]	164 0 0	181 14 0	170 18 0		

KILDARE.

COUNTY OF

[illegible]	Record Number	Date of Order	Name of Tenant.	Name of Landlord.	Poor Law Union.	Townland,
Assistant Commissioners—		1877.				
M. T. Crean (Legal). T. A. Dillon. J. A. O'Kelly.	4325	Apr. 25,	John Lyng, ...	Lady Ashtaly, ...	New Ross, ...	Kilmore, ...
	[illegible]	"	Patrick Bowran, ...	Richard Fleider, ...	do. ...	Listerlin, ...
						Total, ...

KING'S

[illegible]	Record Number	Date of Order	Name of Tenant.	Name of Landlord.	Poor Law Union.	Townland,
Assistant Commissioners— M. T. Crean (Legal). F. M. Carroll. J. Hawkins.	[illegible]	Apr. 5,	Michael King, ...	John H. Going, ...	Roscrea, ...	Rathnaskill, ...

COUNTY OF

[illegible]	Record Number	Date of Order	Name of Tenant.	Name of Landlord.	Poor Law Union.	Townland,
Assistant Commissioners— M. T. Crean (Legal). J. D. Boyd. J. Gernaine.	2496	Apr. 9,	John Jardine, ...	Robert Trimble, ...	Ardee, ...	Paughanstown,
	2497	"	Denis Carolan, ...	T. J. Carolan, ...	do. ...	Arthurstown,
	2498	"	Catherine Lennon,	do. ...	do. ...	do. ...
	2519	"	Laurence Heraty,	Col. R. G. Hamilton, ...	Drogheda, ...	Marthastown,
	[illegible]	"	James Cranny, ...	George C. Smyth, ...	do. ...	Newtownstalaban.
	2311	"	Catherine M'Guigan,	Samuel Bradford, ...	Dundalk, ...	Dungooly, ...
	2310	"	Peter M'Kenna, ...	do. ...	do. ...	do. ...
	[illegible]	"	Patrick Hamill, ...	do. ...	do. ...	do. ...
	[illegible]	"	John Murphy, ...	do. ...	do. ...	do. ...
	[illegible]	"	Patrick Henry, ...	do. ...	do. ...	do. ...
	[illegible]	"	James Keegan, ...	do. ...	do. ...	do. ...
	[illegible]	"	Henry Rice, ...	Maria Wilson and others, Trustees of Estate of Mrs. Elizabeth M'Elwain.	do. ...	Edmondstown, ...
	2504	"	Marian G. Graham,	Blayney R. T. Balfour, ...	do. ...	Tullydrum, ...
	2514	"	John Traynor, ...	John Ryan, ...	do. ...	Lisdoo, ...
	2518	"	Patrick Keenan, ...	W. J. Wilkinson and anor., Trustees of Will of A. G. Keogh, decd.	Ardee, ...	Gunstown, ...
	2516	"	Daniel Byrne, ...	do. ...	do. ...	do. ...
						Total, ...

FIRST STATUTORY TERM.

KILKENNY.

Area of Holding. Statute Measure.	Poor Law Valuation.	Former Rent.	Judicial Rent.	Observations.	Value of Tenancy.
A. R. P.	£ s. d.	£ s. d.	£ s. d.		£ s. d.
60 1 31	34 6 0	64 8 8	30 0 0		
60 1 9	61 15 0	60 0 0	68 0 0		
120 3 0	96 0 0	124 8 8	98 0 0		

COUNTY.

Area of Holding. Statute Measure.	Poor Law Valuation.	Former Rent.	Judicial Rent.	Observations.	Value of Tenancy.
46 1 27	37 0 0	37 0 0	33 18 0		

LOUTH.

Area of Holding. Statute Measure.	Poor Law Valuation.	Former Rent.	Judicial Rent.	Observations.	Value of Tenancy.
7 6 22	5 0 0	7 8 0	4 0 0		
15 1 3	13 0 0	20 0 0	14 0 0		
13 1 23	18 10 0	14 0 0	10 6 0		
18 8 8	10 8 0	15 11 0	9 10 0		
18 0 19	18 5 0	21 0 0	17 15 0		
5 1 39	3 10 0	8 0 0	3 4 0		
0 1 7	1 10 0	1 10 0	1 6 0		
0 0 16	1 0 0	0 16 0	0 15 0		
25 0 14	20 0 0	26 0 0	20 0 0		
6 1 26	3 16 0	4 0 0	3 3 0		
16 6 31	14 0 0	14 0 0	11 10 0		
6 1 36	6 10 0	6 10 0	5 7 6		
94 3 23	83 16 0	130 0 0	91 0 0		

FIRST STATUTORY TERM.

COUNTY OF

Names of Assistant Commissioners by whom Cases were decided.	Record Number.	Date of Decision.	Name of Tenant.	Name of Landlord.	Poor Law Union.	Townland.
Assistant Commissioners—		1897.				
M. T. Crean (Legal). J. D. Boyd J. Gumbleton.	5423	April 9,	James Gammons, ...	Miss F. H. Reynell, ...	Ardee, ...	Lobinstown, ...
	3413	"	Wm. P. Cairnes, ...	Sir E. S. Hutchinson, Bt.,	Drogheda, ...	Colpe, ...
	5405	"	James Warren, ...	Robert P. Maxwell, ...	do. ...	Ballowstown, ...
						Total, ...

QUEEN'S

Names of Assistant Commissioners by whom Cases were decided.	Record Number.	Date of Decision.	Name of Tenant.	Name of Landlord.	Poor Law Union.	Townland.
Assistant Commissioners— M. T. Crean (Legal). F. M. Carroll. J. Hawkes.	3574	April 9,	Robert Pearson, ...	Robert H. Stubber, ...	Roscrea, ...	Clonmore, ...
	3560	"	William Harris, ...	Rev. Sir Algernon Coote, Bart.	Mountmellick	Knocknakearn,
	3572	"	Martin Hogan, ...	John T. Pigott, ...	do. ...	Clonagh, ...
	3561	"	Mrs. Elizabeth Sheane	Earl of Drogheda, ...	do. ...	Towlerton, ...
						Total, ...

COUNTY OF

Names of Assistant Commissioners by whom Cases were decided.	Record Number.	Date of Decision.	Name of Tenant.	Name of Landlord.	Poor Law Union.	Townland.
Assistant Commissioners—	5100	April 23,	Gregory Furlong, Limited Admr. of Edward Daly.	Mrs. L. M. C. S. B. B. Colclough.	New Ross, ...	Yoletown, ...
M. T. Crean (Legal). T. A. Dillon. J. A. O'Kelly.	5102	"	Patrick Hanlon, ...	do.	do. ...	Saltmills, ...
	5150	"	Michael Cousins, ...	do.	do. ...	do. ...
	5101	"	James Barry, ...	do.	do. ...	do. ...
	5113	"	Mark Leary, ...	do.	do. ...	Baley, ...
	5114	"	James Keating, ...	do.	do. ...	do. ...
	5115	"	Mary Hanlon, ...	do.	do. ...	do. ...
	5116	"	John Rossiter, ...	do.	do. ...	do. ...
	5117	"	Catherine Power, ...	do.	do. ...	do. ...
	5118	"	Laurence Cheevers,	do.	do. ...	do. ...
	5119	"	Mary Dwyer, ...	do.	do. ...	do. ...
	5120	"	James Kinsella, ...	do.	do. ...	do. ...
	5121	"	Johanna Whelan, ...	do.	do. ...	do. ...
	5122	"	Thos. Connors, ...	do.	do. ...	do. ...
	5123	"	David Ryan, ...	do.	do. ...	do. ...
	5126	"	John Doyle, ...	do.	do. ...	Garrydaff, ...
	5142	"	Denis Walsh, ...	do.	do. ...	Nash, ...
	5130	"	James Larkin, ...	do.	do. ...	do. ...

FIRST STATUTORY TERM.

MEATH.

Extent of Holding. Statute.	Poor Law Valuation.	Former Rent.	Judicial Rent.	Observations.	Value of Tenancy.
A. R. P.	£ s. d.	£ s. d.	£ s. d.		£ s. d.
71 1 22	23 0 0	25 17 1	19 10 0		
38 0 5	43 0 0	30 0 0	55 0 0		
67 3 28	45 0 0	53 16 0	63 0 0		
177 1 15	190 0 0	189 16 1	137 15 0		

COUNTY.

Extent of Holding. Statute.	Poor Law Valuation.	Former Rent.	Judicial Rent.	Observations.	Value of Tenancy.
19 2 0	18 5 0	16 0 0	13 0 0		
27 0 30	16 15 0	14 11 6	14 0 0		
115 1 22	24 10 0	33 11 11	30 0 0		
10 3 25	6 10 0	24 0 0	15 5 6		
174 0 8	61 0 0	60 3 6	72 11 8		

WEXFORD.

Extent of Holding. Statute.	Poor Law Valuation.	Former Rent.	Judicial Rent.	Observations.	Value of Tenancy.
3 0 34	3 10 0	3 0 0	1 5 0		
8 3 4	8 15 0	8 17 4	7 11 0		
6 0 0	5 0 0	6 11 8	4 8 0		
1 3 0	3 0 0	1 10 0	1 1 0		
23 0 5	16 0 0	30 6 3	9 5 0		
15 0 20	8 0 0	5 0 0	5 5 0		
10 1 0	6 10 0	5 15 5	4 0 0		
7 1 14	5 5 0	4 0 0	3 3 0		
17 5 23	7 15 0	6 0 0	5 5 0		
12 0 17	8 0 0	7 16 3	6 0 0		
34 3 0	19 10 0	16 6 0	11 11 0		
36 1 35	14 0 0	15 14 0	5 17 0		
40 3 0	23 10 0	22 15 0	14 10 0		
43 3 33	34 0 0	37 10 0	24 0 0		
57 3 15	16 15 0	15 15 0	18 10 0		
53 0 31	20 10 0	31 0 0	18 16 6		
27 0 0	11 10 0	14 7 5	9 15 0		
35 3 30	19 15 0	21 3 6	16 0 0		

COUNTY OF

Names of Assistant Commissioners by whom Cases were decided.	Record Number.	Date of Order.	Name of Tenant.	Name of Landlord.	Poor Law Union.	Townland.
Assistant Commissioners—	5129	1897. Apr. 28,	Margaret Sutton, ...	Mrs. L. M. S. C. R. B. Colclough.	New Ross,	Nash, ...
M. T. Craig (Legal). E. A. Dillon. J. A. O'Kelly.	5120	"	John Browne, ...	do.	do. ...	Carrycullen, ...
	5122	"	William Walsh, ...	do.	do. ...	Saint Kearns,
	5145	"	Thomas Browne,	do.	do. ...	do. ...
	5134	"	Thomas A. Murphy,	do.	do. ...	Kinnagh and another.
	5178	"	Joseph Farrell, ...	do.	do. ...	Saint Kearns and another.
	5141	"	John Hardy, ...	do.	do. ...	Milltown, ...
	5103	"	Philip M'Grath, ...	do.	do. ...	Nash, ...
	5123	"	Mrs. Margaret Murphy,	do.	do. ...	do. ...
	5298	"	John Cullen, ...	do.	do. ...	Tinnock, ...
	5104	"	Patrick Stafford, ...	do.	do. ...	Ballyconnor, ...
	5105	"	Jacob Smith, ...	do.	do. ...	do. ...
	5107	"	John Barville, ...	do.	do. ...	do. ...
	5108	"	Johanna Power, ...	do.	do. ...	do. ...
	5109	"	Ellen Flannery, ...	do.	do. ...	do. ...
	5109	"	Patrick Kehoe, ...	do.	do. ...	do. ...
	5110	"	Patrick Flynn, Ltd. Admor. of Mrs. Bridget Hennessy.	do.	do. ...	do. ...
	5111	"	Valentine Ahearne,	do.	do. ...	do. ...
	5112	"	Robert Cardiff, ...	do.	do. ...	do. ...
	5101	"	John Carty, ...	do.	do. ...	Tobarcoo, ...
	5130	"	Catherine Barville,	do.	do. ...	do. ...
	5154	"	Patrick Malloy, ...	do.	do. ...	do. ...
	5132	"	James Michells, ...	do.	do. ...	do. ...
	5136	"	James Ahearne, ...	A. L. Cliffe, ...	do. ...	Baley, ...
	5139	"	Patrick Kinsella, ...	do.	do. ...	do. ...
	5140	"	James Keating, ...	do.	do. ...	do. ...
	5142	"	Patrick Mullen, ...	E. V. W. Richards and others.	Wexford, ...	Rathaspick, ...
	5143	"	David Cullen, ...	do.	do. ...	do. ...
	5144	"	Patrick Murphy, ...	Col. E. P. Pigott, ...	do. ...	Gorey, ...
	5146	"	Francis Bennett, ...	J. J. Percival & another,	do. ...	Haysestown Great.
	5169	"	Thos. Cullen, entd. in the name of James Cullen.	Lady A. Fitzgerald, ...	do. ...	Kilmokea, ...
	5170	"	Michael Leary, ...	do.	do. ...	do. ...
	5137	"	Robert Kinsella, ...	Geo. Fredk. Pierce & anr.,	Enniscorthy,	Ballymackessy.

FIRST STATUTORY TERM.

WEXFORD—*continued.*

Extent of Holding. Statute.	Poor Law Valuation.	Former Rent.	Judicial Rent.	Observations.	Value of Tenancy
A. R. P.	£ s. d.	£ s. d.	£ s. d.		£ s. d.
[illegible] 1 0	11 0 0	12 1 1	20 10 0		
4 3 16	0 15 0	8 0 0	8 8 0		
2 1 [illegible]	3 0 0	2 10 0	1 12 0		
3 0 [illegible]	2 0 0	2 2 0	1 10 0		
31 2 30	20 15 0	[illegible] 0 0	17 0 0		
27 0 0	15 5 0	12 10 6	15 18 4		
3 3 16	3 10 0	5 4 0	2 14 0		
9 1 8	6 0 0	8 0 0	5 15 0		
7 3 8	3 15 0	8 0 0	5 16 0		
2 0 0	1 10 0	2 10 0	1 6 8		
4 1 30	1 10 0	3 0 0	2 0 0		
10 0 26	7 0 0	7 10 0	5 5 0		
13 1 20	5 5 0	8 8 0	4 5 0		
8 3 20	8 0 0	9 10 0	2 2 0		
2 0 4	0 10 0	1 0 0	0 7 6		
6 0 [illegible]	4 0 0	2 0 0	2 12 0		
[illegible] 0 24	10 10 0	19 10 0	8 10 0		
48 2 [illegible]	20 0 0	[illegible] 7 0	17 2 6		
[illegible] 2 34	15 0 0	16 0 0	10 0 0		
4 0 0	8 16 0	3 2 0	8 13 0		
[illegible] 1 10	16 0 0	16 0 0	11 13 0		
4 2 0	8 18 0	4 0 0	3 3 0		
6 3 8	4 10 0	3 16 0	2 10 0		
31 3 8	12 10 0	11 15 6	7 13 0		
14 2 4	7 10 0	7 13 6	4 0 0		
16 2 27	6 0 0	9 4 2	6 0 0		
13 1 [illegible]	7 10 0	7 0 7	6 5 0		
[illegible] 0 12	34 0 0	35 8 10	[illegible] 0 0		
17 1 7	8 0 0	7 8 10	4 10 0		
30 0 30	4 10 0	6 1 0	4 0 0		
64 3 7	19 0 0	19 5 0	13 0 0		
47 1 16	33 10 0	31 0 0	18 0 0		
13 3 8	9 0 0	8 16 11	8 18 11		

FIRST STATUTORY TERM.

COUNTY OF

Names of Assistant Commissioners by whom Cases were decided.	Record Number	Date of Order	Name of Tenant	Name of Landlord	Poor Law Union	Townland
Assistant Commissioners—		1887.				
	5152	Apr. 28,	William Williams,	Rev. E. Stopford Ram,	Gorey, ...	Moneytown & [illegible]
M. T. Crean (Legal). T. A. Dillon. J. A. O'Healy.	5153	„	Moses Doyle, contd. in the name of Morgan Doyle, Adm. of said Moses Doyle.	William O. Forster, ...	do., ...	Sbrule, ...
	5124	„	Henry Tapley, ...	Col. V. L. Hatton, ...	do., ...	Ballingarry, ...
	5165	„	Luke Murdock, ...	do., ...	do., ...	Ballingarry Up.,
	5171	„	Paul Doyle, ...	Andrew Thacker, ...	do., ...	Raley, ...
	5061	„	Moses Byrne, ...	Mrs. J. W. Deane, continued in the name of John Stafford Deane.	New Ross,	Adamstown, ...
						Total, ...

PROVINCE OF

COUNTY OF

Names of Assistant Commissioners by whom Cases were decided.	Record Number	Date of Order	Name of Tenant	Name of Landlord	Poor Law Union	Townland
Assistant Commissioners—	15428	Apr. 25,	Bridget Jennings, ...	Anne Lynch and others,	Ballinrobe, ...	Carrymore, ...
M. T. Crean (Legal). T. A. Dillon. J. A. O'Healy.	15430	„	Michael Slattery, ...	Do., ...	do., ...	Derrymore, ...
	15433	„	John Hynes (Pat),	Do., ...	do., ...	do., ...
	15420	„	Mary Higgins, ...	Major G. W. Vesey, ...	Claremorris,	Scalla, ...
						Total, ...

PROVINCE OF

COUNTY OF

Names of Assistant Commissioners by whom Cases were decided.	Record Number	Date of Order	Name of Tenant	Name of Landlord	Poor Law Union	Townland
Assistant Commissioners—	8577	Mar. 18,	Mary Grady, ...	Miss Alicia O'Connor, ...	Tulla, ...	Ballymacloon,
L. Doyle (Legal). C. O'Keeffe. J. Rice.	8642	Apr. 13,	James Parnell, ...	Lord Annaly, ...	Ballyvaughan,	Glenculanabbey,
	8701	„	Thomas O'Dea, ...	Lord Inchiquin, ...	do., ...	Cahirmore, ...
	8702	„	Bridget O'Dea, ...	do.	do. ...	do. ...
	8619	Mar. 18,	Martin Burns, ...	Francis O'D. B. Foster, a Minor, by T. O'D. B. Foster, his Guardian, and another.	do. ...	Craggagh, ...
						Total, ...

FIRST STATUTORY TERM.

WEXFORD—*continued.*

Area of Holding.	Poor-Law Valuation.	Former Rent.	Judicial Rent.	Observations.	Value of Tenancy.
A. R. P.	£ s. d.	£ s. d.	£ s. d.		£ s. d.
43 0 10	30 10 0	38 10 0	30 0 0		
81 1 38	68 15 0	55 0 0	42 10 0		
15 1 20	15 5 8	14 5 4	9 0 0		
23 0 6	22 5 0	24 0 0	18 10 0		
116 1 8	62 5 0	73 0 0	45 10 0		
6 1 26	3 10 0	2 16 0	2 2 6		
1,135 8 31	780 0 0	783 2 10	537 0 11		

CONNAUGHT.

MAYO.

Area of Holding.	Poor-Law Valuation.	Former Rent.	Judicial Rent.	Observations.	Value of Tenancy.
24 0 18	9 10 0	10 15 0	7 10 0		
7 3 26	6 16 0	5 4 5	4 15 0	With an undivided ⅛th of 11 acres.	
7 3 36	5 4 0	5 8 6	4 0 0	With an undivided ⅛th of 8 acres.	
102 3 6	54 10 0	106 0 0	70 0 0		
146 2 17	76 0 0	135 5 1	86 5 0		

MUNSTER.

CLARE.

FIRST STATUTORY TERM.

COUNTY OF

Names of Assistant Commissioners by whom Cases were decided.	Record Number.	Date of Order.	Name of Tenant.	Name of Landlord.	Poor Law Union.	Townland.
Assistant Commissioners—		1887.				
L. Doyle (Legal). E. O. Fury.	15304	Apr. 8,	James Morrison, ...	Jane H. C. Healy, wife of John Henry Healy.	Midleton, ...	Kilbrack, ...
	15673	"	Robert Parker, ...	Viscount Midleton, ...	do., ...	Broomfield, West,
	15377	"	Maurice Hegarty,	do., ...	do., ...	Coppingerstown
	15663	"	Robert Parker, ...	do., ...	do., ...	Townparks, ...
	15696	"	Thomas Brien, ...	do., ...	do., ...	Castleredmond,
	15570	"	Patrick Rourke, ...	do., ...	do., ...	[illegible]
	15615	"	Ellen Neill, ...	William Collins, ...	do., ...	[illegible] West,
	15551	"	Edmund Ahern, ...	Captain E. B. M'Bride,	do., ...	[illegible]
						Total, ...

COUNTY OF

Names of Assistant Commissioners by whom Cases were decided.	Record Number.	Date of Order.	Name of Tenant.	Name of Landlord.	Poor Law Union.	Townland.
Assistant Commissioners—	7263	Apr. 9,	Margaret Donahoe,	Joseph Griffith, ...	Roscrea, ...	Kilnas, ...
M. T. Crean (Legal). F. M. Carroll. J. Hawkins.	7262	"	John Corrigan, ...	Maria Kennedy & others,	do., ...	[illegible], ...
						Total, ...

CIVIL BILL

PROVINCE OF

COUNTY OF

CORK.

Extent of Holding. Statute.			Poor Law Valuation.			Former Rent.			Judicial Rent.			Observations.	Value of Tenancy.		
A.	R.	P.	£	s.	d.	£	s.	d.	£	s.	d.		£	s.	d.
64	3	23	30	0	0	30	0	0	27	7	4				
6	0	30	6	5	0	8	0	0	6	0	0				
10	0	0	5	10	0	12	10	0	9	7	6				
8	2	10	13	15	0	23	17	8	15	10	0				
17	1	0	13	10	0	22	0	0	12	5	0				
39	3	35	34	5	0	41	16	0	31	5	0				
2	1	29	3	0	0	3	10	0	2	12	0				
77	2	31	48	10	0	49	7	0	43	17	6				
226	1	2	157	16	0	193	0	8	148	4	6				

TIPPERARY.

A.	R.	P.	£	s.	d.	£	s.	d.	£	s.	d.	Observations.	Value of Tenancy.
12	0	23	9	0	0	13	0	0	8	16	0		
6	1	30	12	0	0	13	0	0	9	11	0		
19	2	9	21	0	0	26	0	0	18	6	0		

COURTS.

ULSTER.

CAVAN.

Extent of Holding. Statute.			Poor Law Valuation.			Former Rent.			Judicial Rent.			Observations.	Value of Tenancy.		
A.	R.	P.	£	s.	d.	£	s.	d.	£	s.	d.		£	s.	d.
19	1	28	12	5	0	11	15	7	8	10	0				
4	1	0	6	5	0	7	0	0	5	10	0				
2	0	7	2	0	0	3	14	4	2	5	0				
25	2	35	20	10	0	22	12	11	16	5	0				

FIRST STATUTORY TERM.

PROVINCE OF

COUNTY OF

County Court Judge.	Record Number.	Date of Order.	Name of Tenant.	Name of Landlord.	Poor Law Union.	Townland.
		1887.				
D. FitzGerald, Q.C.	581	Jan. 13,	William Williams,	Robert Tyndall, ...	Waterford,	Milltown, ...
	582	"	Edmund Dunphy, ...	do.	do. ...	do. ...
	583	"	James M'Donald,	do.	do. ...	do. ...
	584	"	Philip Hartnessy,	do.	do. ...	do. ...
	585	"	John Quinn, ...	do.	do. ...	do. ...
	586	"	James Quinn, ...	do.	do. ...	do. ...
	587	"	Wm. Rockett, ...	do.	do. ...	do. ...
	592	"	Peter Phelan, ...	do.	do. ...	do. ...
	610	Apr. 15,	Thomas Martin, ...	Mrs. H. M. Usher, ...	Thomastown,	Bennett's Bridge.
	611	"	James Brophy, ...	Martin Scurry, ...	do. ...	Killeen, ...
	609	"	Thomas Grant, ...	Gwynne Dyer and anor.,	do. ...	Kilkenny, ...
	608	"	Johanna Moylan,	Rev. P. J. Mulhall and another, Trustees of R. Lyons, deceased.	do. ...	Knightsown, ...
	607	"	Thomas Byrne, ...	do.	do. ...	do. ...
	606	"	James Kinsey, ...	do.	do. ...	do. ...
	605	"	Johanna Brennan	do.	do. ...	do. ...
	603	"	Anne Connors, ...	Miss Mary Maher, ...	Kilkenny,	Shanganagh's Castle.
	602	"	John Rohan, ...	Sir J. J. Coghill, Bart.,	do. ...	Kilmogue, ...
	597	"	Nicholas O'Donnell,	Mrs. Bridget Fenton, ...	Thomastown,	Killeen West
	596	"	James Kirwan, ...	Joseph O'N. Power, ...	Waterford,	Ballyrahan, ...
	582	"	Pierce Fleming, ...	Edward N. Twopenny,	Callan, ...	Kilree, ...
						Third, ...

COUNTY OF

County Court Judge.	Record Number.	Date of Order.	Name of Tenant.	Name of Landlord.	Poor Law Union.	Townland.
W. H. Kisbey, Q.C.	337	Apr. 14,	Joseph Lennon, ...	Lord Roden, ...	Dundalk, ...	South Marsh
	344	"	Richard Reddy, ...	do.	do. ...	do. ...
	347	"	Owen Treanor, ...	Major Lake, ...	do. ...	[illegible] (Murphy).
	346	"	Peter M'Bride, ...	St. Clair K. M. Stobart,	do. ...	Clermont, ...

FIRST STATUTORY TERM.

LEINSTER.

KILKENNY.

Extent of Holding. Statute.	Poor Law Valuation.	Former Rent.	Judicial Rent.	Observations.	Value of Tenancy.
A. R. P.	£ s. d.	£ s. d.	£ s. d.		£ s. d.
[illegible] 2 [illegible]	[illegible] 0 0	42 0 0	30 0 0		
30 3 21	39 0 0	47 0 0	32 10 0		
60 0 [illegible]	61 0 0	74 0 0	[illegible] 0 0		
13 0 31	14 10 0	18 10 0	12 10 0		
20 1 [illegible]	27 0 0	30 0 0	21 10 0		
[illegible] 2 31	[illegible] 0 0	60 0 0	31 10 0		
[illegible] 0 18	77 0 0	107 10 0	73 0 0		
47 3 6	40 0 0	64 10 0	44 0 0		
[illegible] 3 14	[illegible] 0 0	65 4 0	37 10 0		
26 0 [illegible]	25 0 0	34 0 0	21 10 0		
36 1 [illegible]	13 0 0	16 0 0	11 0 0		
19 0 34	10 14 0	11 18 9	7 0 0		
[illegible] 0 [illegible]	25 0 0	[illegible] 0 0	17 0 0		
6 4 24	7 10 0	10 0 0	7 10 0		
33 1 23	24 0 0	37 0 0	17 4 0		
4 0 11	[illegible]	12 4 2	9 12 0		
34 0 7	19 10 0	[illegible] 0 0	17 10 0		
123 0 22	66 6 0	73 11 0	49 0 0		
[illegible] 1 16	44 10 0	61 10 10	46 0 0		
[illegible] 0 0	[illegible] 10 0	[illegible] 0 0	23 0 0		
613 0 9	708 10 0	874 7 7	666 2 0		

COUNTY OF

Name of County Court Judge.	Record Number.	Date of Order.	Name of Tenant.	Name of Landlord.	Poor Law Union.	Townland.
		1897.				
W. H. Kisbey, Q.C.	249	Apr. 24,	Peter M'Geown, ...	St. Clair K. M. Stobart,	Dundalk, ...	[illegible], ...
	250	"	Matthew M'Bride,	do.	do. ...	do. ...
	241	"	John M'Geown,	do.	do. ...	do. ...
	257	"	Terence M'Geown,	do.	do. ...	do. ...
	245	"	Ellen Trainor, Repr. of Mary M'Geown.	do.	do. ...	do. ...
						Total, ...

QUEEN'S

Name of County Court Judge.	Record Number.	Date of Order.	Name of Tenant.	Name of Landlord.	Poor Law Union.	Townland.
D. Fitzgerald, Q.C.	230	Apr. 10,	John Butler, ...	Rev. William Dowdall,	Roscrea, ...	Derryvorrigan,
	246	"	Patrick Devoy, ...	Thomas Lowman, ...	Athy, ...	Ballyadams, ...
	276	"	Anne Seeley, ...	James Flach, ...	Abbeyleix,	Graigue, ...
	267	"	Langley Thompson,	Mrs. M. E. Lalor, ...	Roscrea, ...	Kyleclonfinn,
						Total, ...

COUNTY OF

Name of County Court Judge.	Record Number.	Date of Order.	Name of Tenant.	Name of Landlord.	Poor Law Union.	Townland.
R. S. Hare.	56	Apr. 24,	Hannah Evans and another.	Francis La Touche, ...	Rathdrum, ...	Rathdown, Lr.,

PROVINCE OF

COUNTY OF

Name of County Court Judge.	Record Number.	Date of Order.	Name of Tenant.	Name of Landlord.	Poor Law Union.	Townland.
W. S. [illegible], Q.C.	2917	Jan. 21,	Timothy Carey, ...	Cornelius F. [illegible], ...	Clonakilty,	[illegible],
	2922	"	Thomas M'Grath, ...	Rev. Thomas J. Halloran,	Bandon, ...	Kilbrogan, ...
	2940	"	John Foley, ...	Maurice Frewen, ...	do. ...	Carrigcannon,
	2902	"	Edward Barrett, ...	Francis E. Rowland, ...	do. ...	Ballynamuddagh,
	2901	"	Do. ...	do. ...	do. ...	do. ...
	2799	Feb. 1,	Michael Whelahan,	R. H. E. White, ...	Bantry, ...	Ardnageehy Beg.
	2237	Jan. 22,	Cornelius Sullivan,	Jasper K. Peck, ...	Dunmanway,	Clash, ...
	2906	"	Daniel Driscoll, ...	Mrs. Emma Beamish, ...	Clonakilty,	Ahagilla, ...
						Total, ...

LOUTH—*continued.*

Extent of Holdings.	Poor Law Valuation.	Present Rent.	Judicial Rent.	Observations.	Value of Tenancy.
A. R. P.	£ s. d.	£ s. d.	£ s. d.		£ s. d.
16 1 4	8 16 0	6 13 6	8 16 6		
21 1 17	7 5 0	8 6 1	6 0 0		
19 1 34	7 0 0	6 7 6	5 8 0		
20 1 15	8 0 0	7 10 3	6 7 6		
15 3 16	5 2 0	4 3 6	3 10 0		
149 2 13	94 18 0	80 0 8	70 15 3		

COUNTY.

65 3 30	35 0 0	29 16 6	31 10 0		
16 3 38	11 8 0	11 0 0	6 0 0		
19 2 6	13 0 0	12 10 0	8 0 0		
20 1 33	20 0 0	22 0 0	17 0 0		
118 0 34	79 8 0	65 6 6	64 10 0		

WICKLOW.

3 0 20	[illegible]	6 1 6	5 14 0		

MUNSTER.

CORK.

34 3 34	16 0 0	16 0 0	13 0 0		
3 1 30	5 0 0	4 10 0	3 3 0		
15 0 10	3 0 0	13 10 0	8 18 0		
27 3 7	24 15 0	26 0 0	20 0 0		
28 1 25	11 10 0	15 0 0	10 0 0		
19 1 13	6 10 0	5 0 0	5 0 0		
91 0 33	53 0 0	66 0 0	40 5 0		
26 2 34	39 10 0	30 4 0	34 17 6		
246 1 29	158 5 0	150 4 0	176 1 6		

FIRST STATUTORY TERM.

COUNTY OF KERRY.

[illegible]	[illegible]	[illegible]	[illegible]	[illegible]	[illegible]	[illegible]	[illegible]	[illegible]	[illegible]	[illegible]	[illegible]	[illegible]
		[illegible]					£ s. d.	£ s. d.	£ s. d.	£ s. d.		£ s. d.
[illegible], Q.C.	[illegible]	Jan. [illegible]	[illegible]	[illegible]	[illegible]	[illegible]	[illegible]	[illegible]	[illegible]	[illegible]		
	[illegible]	Feb. [illegible]	[illegible]	[illegible]	[illegible]	[illegible]	[illegible]	[illegible]	[illegible]	[illegible]		
	[illegible]	Jan. [illegible]	[illegible]	[illegible]	[illegible]	[illegible]	[illegible]	[illegible]	[illegible]	[illegible]		
	[illegible]	Feb. [illegible]	[illegible]	[illegible]	[illegible]	[illegible]	[illegible]	[illegible]	[illegible]	[illegible]		
	[illegible]	„	[illegible]	[illegible]	[illegible]	[illegible]	[illegible]	[illegible]	[illegible]	[illegible]		
	[illegible]	Jan. [illegible]	[illegible]	[illegible]	[illegible]	[illegible]	[illegible]	[illegible]	[illegible]	[illegible]		
	[illegible]	Feb. [illegible]	[illegible]	[illegible]	[illegible]	[illegible]	[illegible]	[illegible]	[illegible]	[illegible]		
	[illegible]	Jan. [illegible]	[illegible]	[illegible]	[illegible]	[illegible]	[illegible]	[illegible]	[illegible]	[illegible]		
	[illegible]	Feb. [illegible]	[illegible]	[illegible]	[illegible]	[illegible]	[illegible]	[illegible]	[illegible]	[illegible]		
						Total, ..	[illegible]	[illegible]	[illegible]	[illegible]		

CIVIL BILL COURTS.

COUNTY OF LIMERICK.

[illegible], Q.C.	[illegible]	Jan. [illegible]	[illegible]	[illegible]	[illegible]	[illegible]	[illegible]	[illegible]	[illegible]	[illegible]		

Printed image digitised by the University of Southampton Library Digitisation Unit

LAND LAW (IRELAND) ACT, 1896.

FIRST STATUTORY TERM.

LEASEHOLDERS.

FIRST STATUTORY TERM.

PROVINCE OF

COUNTY OF

Names of Assistant Commissioners by whom Cases were decided.	Record Number.	Date of Order.	Name of Tenant.	Name of Landlord.	Poor Law Union.	Townland.
Chief Commissioner.	9676	1887 April 29,	John Thompson, ...	Colonel E. D. Leslie, ...	Ballymoney.	Moyarrig, Upper

COUNTY OF

Names of Assistant Commissioners by whom Cases were decided.	Record Number.	Date of Order.	Name of Tenant.	Name of Landlord.	Poor Law Union.	Townland.
Assistant Commissioners— J. H. Edge (Legal). F. O'Callaghan. L. Carbery.	7484	April 7,	Thomas Harris, ...	Major Hy. Ed. Maxwell,	Cavan, ...	Corbagh, ...

COUNTY OF

Names of Assistant Commissioners by whom Cases were decided.	Record Number.	Date of Order.	Name of Tenant.	Name of Landlord.	Poor Law Union.	Townland.
Assistant Commissioners— W. F. Bailey (Legal). S. Byrne. Thomas Roberts.	12083	April 14,	Wm. John Cowan,	Lieut.-Col. Alexander, ...	Banbridge, ...	Coppy, ...

COUNTY OF

Names of Assistant Commissioners by whom Cases were decided.	Record Number.	Date of Order.	Name of Tenant.	Name of Landlord.	Poor Law Union.	Townland.
Assistant Commissioners— C. H. Tyrrell (Legal). A. R. Montgomery. R. W. Gradwell.	12869	Mar. 23,	James Wilson, contd. in name of Newberry Wilson.	Mrs. Amy H. M'Clintock,	Omagh, ...	Drumconnell, ...
	12877	"	Samuel Moore, contd. in name of John Moore.	do. ...	do. ...	do. ...
J. H. Edge (Legal). J. Howlin. W. Small.	12916	Mar. 31,	Robert H. Dickson,	Earl of Caledon, ...	Dungannon,	Kilnacart, ...
	12944	"	Samuel J. Coddon,	do.	do. ...	[illegible] ...

ULSTER.

ANTRIM.

Extent of Holding—Statute.	Poor Law Valuation.	Former Rent.	Judicial Rent.	Observations.	Value of Tenancy.
A. R. P.	£ s. d.	£ s. d.	£ s. d.		£ s. d.
[illegible] 3 18	20 0 0	19 18 6	19 0 0	The rent in this case was fixed by consent of the parties at the sitting of the Court in Dublin.	

CAVAN.

Extent of Holding—Statute.	Poor Law Valuation.	Former Rent.	Judicial Rent.	Observations.	Value of Tenancy.
[illegible] 1 33	[illegible] 0 0	25 0 0	15 15 0		

DOWN.

Extent of Holding—Statute.	Poor Law Valuation.	Former Rent.	Judicial Rent.	Observations.	Value of Tenancy.
24 1 7	[illegible] 0 0	45 0 0	[illegible] 0 0		

TYRONE.

FIRST STATUTORY TERM.

COUNTY OF

Names of Assistant Commissioners [illegible]	Record Number.	Date of Order.	Name of Tenant.	Name of Landlord.	Poor Law Union.	Townland.
Assistant Commissioners—		1897				
C. H. Tarleton (Legal). G. N. Callaghan. W. H. Hume.	12823	Mar. 30,	John Kane, ...	Archibald M'D. Elliott,	Strabane, ...	Stonyvalle and [illegible].
	12458	"	James Marshall, ...	do. ...	do. ...	Stonyvalle, ...
	12460	"	George Kane and another.	do.	do. ...	Clardy Holi-day.
	12833	"	Patrick Cassidy Rep. of Felix Cassidy.	Miss Isabella M'Farlane,	do. ...	Carnamoney, ...
						Total ...

PROVINCE OF

COUNTY OF

Names of Assistant Commissioners	Record Number.	Date of Order.	Name of Tenant.	Name of Landlord.	Poor Law Union.	Townland.
Assistant Commissioners— L. Doyle (Legal). A. F. Cowen. G. S. Ralston.	1633	Apr. 26,	Mary Ann Dowdall,	Anne Emma Maria Baker and ano., Minors by Anne Osborne, their Guardian.	Balrothery,	Oldtown [illegible], ...

KING'S

Names of Assistant Commissioners	Record Number.	Date of Order.	Name of Tenant.	Name of Landlord.	Poor Law Union.	Townland.
Assistant Commissioners. M. T. Cuban (Legal). F. M. Carroll. J. Hawkins.	3264	Apr. 9,	George Larke, ...	Benjamin P. Smallman,	Mountmellick.	Rapheen, ...

QUEEN'S

Names of Assistant Commissioners	Record Number.	Date of Order.	Name of Tenant.	Name of Landlord.	Poor Law Union.	Townland.
Assistant Commissioners— M. T. Cuban (Legal). F. M. Carroll. J. Hawkins.	3267	Apr. 9,	Samuel Deverill, ...	William Kennedy, ...	Mountmellick.	Mellick, ...
	3246	"	James Dowling, ...	William Fleming Kennedy	Abbeyleix, ...	Pigrim Hill ...
	3307	"	Jeremiah Shelley, Exor. of Will of Hugh O'Kelly, deceased.	Annabella F. Despey, ...	Roscrea, ...	Sentry Hill, ...
	3584	"	Fanny Adelaide Cassan.	Emily Alice Des Voeux,	Mountmellick.	Kilnacourt [illegible]
						Total ...

COUNTY OF

Names of Assistant Commissioners	Record Number.	Date of Order.	Name of Tenant.	Name of Landlord.	Poor Law Union.	Townland.
Assistant Commissioners— M. T. Cuban (Legal). T. A. Dillon. J. A. O'Keeffe.	5209	Apr. 28,	Miss Marion H. Burnside.	Major Henry A. H. Boyse.	Wexford ...	Cullenstown.

FIRST STATUTORY TERM.

TYRONE—*continued.*

Extent of Holding, Statute.	Poor Law Valuation.	Former Rent.	Judicial Rent.	Observations.	Value of Tenancy.
A. R. P.	£ s. d.	£ s. d.	£ s. d.		£ s. d.
13 1 30	25 0 0	27 10 0	21 0 0		
22 3 10	13 0 0	14 0 0	11 0 0		
48 0 20	25 0 0	27 10 0	21 0 0		
13 2 15	4 1 0	2 15 1	2 2 0		
244 0 5	155 15 0	107 15 5	127 14 8		

LEINSTER.

DUBLIN.

91 0 15	75 0 0	91 5 5	55 0 0		

COUNTY.

65 0 19	unascertained,	29 10 0	12 0 0		

FIRST STATUTORY TERM.

PROVINCE OF

COUNTY OF

Names of Assistant Commissioners by whom Cases were decided.	Record Number.	Date of Order.	Name of Tenant.	Name of Landlord.	Poor Law Union.	Townland.
Assistant Commissioners—		1897				
L. Doyle (Legal). G. O'Keeffe. J. Rice.	5844	Apr. 3,	John Burke & anor.,	Lady Fitzgerald, ...	Ennistymon,	Luck, ...
	[illegible]	"	John O'Loghlen (Peter).	Mary G. [illegible] & anor.,	do., ...	Ballyteemaly,
	[illegible]	Apr. 13,	Do., ...	do., ...	Ballyvaughan	[illegible], ...
						Total, ...

COUNTY OF

Names of Assistant Commissioners by whom Cases were decided.	Record Number.	Date of Order.	Name of Tenant.	Name of Landlord.	Poor Law Union.	Townland.
Assistant Commissioners—						
L. Doyle (Legal). Edward Fort.	[illegible]	Apr. 9,	Thomas J. [illegible],	Jeremiah J. M'Daniel, ...	Cork, ...	Carrigaline,
	[illegible]	"	Mary Murphy, ...	Juliana Martin, ...	Midleton,	[illegible], ...
	[illegible]	"	James Morrison, ...	Mrs. Charlotte [illegible],	do., ...	Ballygibbon, ...
	[illegible]	"	Johanna Shea, ...	do., ...	do., ...	do., ...
	[illegible]	"	Mary Higgins, ...	Daniel Cronin, ...	do., ...	Ballinacurra, ...
						Total, ...

COUNTY OF

FIRST STATUTORY TERM.

MUNSTER.

CLARE.

Extent of Holding. Statute.	Poor Law Valuation.	Former Rent.	Judicial Rent.	Observations.	Value of Tenancy.
A. R. P.	£ s. d.	£ s. d.	£ s. d.		£ s. d.
21 0 18	8 10 0	19 5 0	7 2 0		
18 1 21	18 0 0	17 0 0	14 10 0		
54 0 34	12 0 0	25 0 0	20 0 0		
90 2 33	38 10 0	61 5 0	41 12 0		

CORK.

168 0 15	212 16 0	270 0 0	233 0 0		
107 2 8	60 0 0	89 0 0	67 10 0		
32 3 6	19 0 0	81 0 0	17 0 0		
68 2 28	17 15 0	83 0 0	17 10 0		
37 1 8	31 18 0	43 0 0	28 2 6		
413 1 25	351 8 0	600 0 0	343 2 6		

TIPPERARY.

CIVIL BILL COURTS.

PROVINCE OF LEINSTER

FIRST STATUTORY TERM

COUNTY OF KILKENNY.

[illegible]	[illegible]	[illegible]	[illegible]	[illegible]	[illegible]	[illegible]	[illegible]	[illegible]	[illegible]	[illegible]	[illegible]	[illegible]
[illegible]	[illegible]	[illegible]	[illegible]	[illegible]	[illegible]	[illegible]	[illegible]	[illegible]	[illegible]	[illegible]		[illegible]
	[illegible]	[illegible]	[illegible]	[illegible]	[illegible]	[illegible]	[illegible]	[illegible]	[illegible]	[illegible]		
						Total,	[illegible]	[illegible]	[illegible]	[illegible]		

COUNTY OF LOUTH.

[illegible]	[illegible]	[illegible]	[illegible]	[illegible]	[illegible]	[illegible]	[illegible]	[illegible]	[illegible]	[illegible]		

QUEEN'S COUNTY

[illegible]	[illegible]	[illegible]	[illegible]	[illegible]	[illegible]	[illegible]	[illegible]	[illegible]	[illegible]	[illegible]		

MONTH OF APRIL, 1897.

SECOND STATUTORY TERM.

SECOND STATUTORY TERM.

PROVINCE OF

COUNTY OF

[illegible]	Record Number	Date of Order.	Name of Tenant.	Name of Landlord.	Poor Law Union.	Townland.
Assistant Commissioners—		189[illegible].				
D. [illegible] (Legal). T. [illegible]. C. H. [illegible].	[illegible]	Apr. 1,	David Adams, ...	Martin Smyth, Committee of Margaret Dunmath(?), a lunatic.	Ballymena(?),	Killoorey(?), ...
	[illegible]	"	James Stevenson, ...	do.	do. ...	do. ...
	[illegible]	"	Samuel M'Mullen,	do.	do. ...	do. ...
	[illegible]	"	Rose Anne Young,	do.	do. ...	do. ...
	[illegible]	"	Thomas Crompton, ...	do.	do. ...	do. ...
	[illegible]	"	John Robinson, ...	do.	do. ...	do. ...
	[illegible]	"	William Kerr, ...	do.	do. ...	do. ...
	[illegible]	"	Alexander Russell,	do.	do. ...	do. ...
	279	"	John Kerr, ...	do.	do. ...	do. ...
	[illegible]	"	Thomas Crompton, ...	do.	do. ...	do. ...
	[illegible]	"	Arthur M'Laughlin,	do.	do. ...	do. ...
	[illegible]	"	George Kinwin(?), ...	do.	do. ...	do. ...
	274	"	Andrew Kennedy,	do.	do. ...	do. ...
	[illegible]	"	John J. Adams, ...	do.	do. ...	[illegible], ...
	[illegible]	Apr. 14,	Michael M'Keown(?),	George T. Graham, ...	do. ...	[illegible], ...
	[illegible]	"	John Elliott, ...	John M'Ilroy, ...	do. ...	[illegible], ...
	[illegible]	"	James M'Vicker, ...	do.	do. ...	do. ...
	317	"	Patrick Duffin, ...	Harold W. S. Gray, ...	do. ...	[illegible], ...
	316	"	James Donnelly, ...	do.	do. ...	do. ...
	315	"	Patrick Mooney(?), ...	do.	do. ...	do. ...
	316	"	Charles Duffin, ...	do.	do. ...	do. ...
	[illegible]	"	Randal M'Keown(?),	do.	do. ...	do. ...
	[illegible]	"	Mary M'Donnell, ...	do.	do. ...	[illegible],
	[illegible]	"	Michael Doherty, ...	do.	do. ...	do. ...
	218	"	Do. ...	do.	do. ...	do. ...
	211	"	Patrick Reid, ...	do.	do. ...	do. ...
	[illegible]	"	Mary Walsh, ...	do.	do. ...	[illegible],

SECOND STATUTORY TERM.

ULSTER.

ANTRIM.

Extent of Holding. Statute Measure.	Poor Law Valuation.	Rent of Holding prior to commencement of First Statutory Term.	Judicial Rent for First Statutory Term.	Judicial Rent for Second Statutory Term.	Record No. First Statutory Term.	Observations.
A. R. P.	£ s. d.	£ s. d.	£ s. d.	£ s. d.		
12 1 6	[illegible] 16 0	[illegible] 10 0	37 15 0	17 0 0	13	
47 3 [illegible]	[illegible] 10 0	45 10 7	48 16 0	[illegible] 7 0	687	
30 2 0	[illegible] 0 0	[illegible] 16 0	[illegible] 0 0	13 10 0	19	
30 3 14	[illegible] 0 0	[illegible] 10 0	[illegible] 0 0	19 4 0	[illegible]	
9 0 0	6 15 0	9 0 0	7 0 0	8 15 0	[illegible]	
[illegible] 5 31	[illegible] 10 0	23 8 6	17 0 0	10 0 0	486	
30 0 [illegible]	25 16 0	[illegible] 15 0	[illegible] 15 0	14 11 0	[illegible]	
[illegible] 1 6	17 6 6	[illegible] 16 0	[illegible] 16 0	11 3 0	[illegible]	
10 8 10	[illegible] 15 0	31 16 0	21 16 0	16 12 0	679	
44 0 0	[illegible] 5 6	54 10 0	42 0 0	[illegible] 18 0	684	
[illegible] 1 12	31 10 0	33 8 10	[illegible] 17 10	[illegible] 14 6	81	
[illegible] 0 0	[illegible] 18 0	[illegible] 0 0	[illegible] 10 0	15 11 6	681	
46 0 0	[illegible] 10 0	67 0 0	[illegible] 0 0	[illegible] 7 0	478	
[illegible] 3 0	[illegible] 0 0	100 0 0	[illegible] 0 0	[illegible] 7 6	[illegible]	
41 0 0	[illegible] 0 0	77 18 9	[illegible] 14 0	11 0 0	[illegible]	
[illegible] 0 16	[illegible] 5 0	33 0 4	[illegible] 10 0	17 0 0	1117	
[illegible] 2 [illegible]	[illegible] 0 0	36 18 0	20 0 0	[illegible] 10 0	1170	
[illegible] 2 3	14 19 0	24 1 6	18 0 0	10 15 0	[illegible]	With 5 acres on [illegible] and right of cutting turf.
[illegible] 0 12	11 15 0	16 10 0	18 0 0	7 0 0	[illegible]	With [illegible] acres on [illegible] and right of cutting turf.
15 3 0	6 0 0	10 11 0	[illegible]	5 0 0	[illegible]	With [illegible] acres on [illegible] and right of cutting turf.
13 3 7	7 17 0	11 1 0	[illegible]	6 0 0	[illegible]	With [illegible] acres on [illegible] and right of cutting turf.
13 3 6	6 7 0	11 0 0	8 0 0	4 10 0	[illegible]	With [illegible] acres on [illegible] and right of cutting turf.
17 0 31	11 10 0	10 1 4	13 0 0	8 17 6	[illegible]	
13 0 11	5 16 0	9 0 0	6 10 0	4 11 0	[illegible]	
18 2 20	4 0 0	6 10 0	7 0 0	4 7 0	[illegible]	
10 1 25	5 0 0	7 4 6	5 6 0	3 0 0	[illegible]	
10 1 13	unascertained	5 0 0	4 0 0	3 0 0	1003	

SECOND STATUTORY TERM

COUNTY OF

Names of Assistant Commissioners by whom Cases were decided.	Record Number.	Date of Order.	Name of Tenant.	Name of Landlord.	Poor Law Union.	Townland.
Assistant Commissioners—		1897.				
	[illegible]	Apr. 14,	Mathew Reid, ...	Harold W. S. Gray, ...	Ballymena,	Knockanally,
D. Tuomey (Legal). T. Davidson. C. H. Reeves.	919	"	Patrick M'Caughan,	do. ...	do. ...	do. ...
	918	"	John Donnelly, ...	do.	do. ...	do. ...
	910	"	John Duffin, ...	do.	do. ...	do. ...
	[illegible]	"	Patrick Duffin, ...	do.	do. ...	do. ...
	907	"	John Duffin, ...	do.	do. ...	do. ...
	916	"	Daniel Duffin, ...	do.	do. ...	do. ...
	[illegible]	"	Patrick Madden, ...	do.	do. ...	do. ...
	255	"	James Nelson, ...	William Chaine, ...	Larne, ...	Ballytober, ...
	234	"	James M'Cluggage,	do.	do. ...	do. ...
	234	"	Hugh Hamm, ...	George M'Auliffe and another.	do. ...	North West Ballygarry.
	239	"	Edward Hunter, ...	do.	do. ...	do. ...
	[illegible]	"	James M'Creedy, ...	Harold W. S. Gray, ...	Ballymena,	Knockanally,
						Total, ...

COUNTY OF

Names of Assistant Commissioners by whom Cases were decided.	Record Number.	Date of Order.	Name of Tenant.	Name of Landlord.	Poor Law Union.	Townland.
Assistant Commissioners—	734	Apr. 14,	William Hart, ...	Thomas M. H. Chambers,	Newry, ...	Ashvall, ...
W. F. Bailey (Legal). W. Weldon. G. M. Harvey.	746	"	Patrick Kearney, Admor. of Thomas Kearney.	do.	do. ...	Annalis,
	737	"	Michael O'Hare, ...	do.	do. ...	do.
	733	"	Patrick Murphy, ...	do.	do. ...	Ashvall, ...
	736	"	Stephen Hughes, ...	do.	do. ...	do. ...
	767	"	Stephen Green, ...	do.	do. ...	do.
	760	"	Thomas Ferguson, ...	do.	do. ...	do. ...
	719	"	William Hart, ...	do.	do. ...	do. ...
	715	"	Michael Murphy, ...	do.	do. ...	do. ...
	718	"	Bridget Murphy, ...	M. S. Synnot, a lunatic, in Chancery.	do. ...	Carrowmaddy, ...
	631	"	Edward Magennis,	Joseph Wilson, ...	do. ...	Drumbanagh, ...
	620	"	James Donnelly, ...	do.	do. ...	Lisnalee, ...
	485	"	John Elliott, senior,	do.	do. ...	do. ...
	479	"	Henry Donnelly, ...	do.	do. ...	do. ...

SECOND STATUTORY TERM.

ANTRIM—*continued.*

Extent of Holding, Statute.	Poor Law Valuation.	Rent of Holding prior to creation of First Statutory Term.	Judicial Rent for First Statutory Term.	Judicial Rent for Second Statutory Term.	Record No., First Statutory Term.	Observations.
A. R. P.	£ s. d.	£ s. d.	£ s. d.	£ s. d.		
11 0 11	6 6 0	9 15 0	8 15 0	6 10 0	1030	With 5½ acres on mountain.
14 3 3	10 15 0	15 10 0	11 0 0	7 13 0	979	do. 3 acres do.
23 3 30	16 0 0	20 10 0	16 5 0	8 18 0	958	do. 3½ acres do.
18 1 17	11 10 0	17 10 0	11 10 0	7 2 6	985	do. 3 acres do.
19 1 19	13 5 0	15 0 0	15 15 0	9 13 0	985	do. 3 acres do.
17 1 35	9 5 0	12 10 0	10 0 0	7 0 0	956	do. 2½ acres do.
15 2 5	9 0 0	14 0 0	10 5 0	6 5 0	981	do. 6 acres do.
21 1 34	15 5 0	25 0 0	15 5 0	10 0 0	990	do. 8 acres do.
80 1 19	55 10 0	90 0 0	82 0 0	35 7 6	1121	
64 1 0	50 0 0	83 0 0	54 0 0	43 5 0	1128	
34 3 26	34 18 0	23 15 0	22 0 0	16 18 0	197	
18 0 32	15 0 0	18 10 0	18 0 0	11 0 0	190	
11 2 15	7 10 0	11 0 0	8 0 0	4 10 0	983	1½ acres on mountain.
1,095 1 25	[illegible] 5 0	1,071 14 8	634 18 10	810 1 8		

ARMAGH.

SECOND STATUTORY TERM.

COUNTY OF

Names of Assistant Commissioners by whom Cases were decided.	Record Number.	Date of Order.	Name of Tenant.	Name of Landlord.	Poor Law Union.	Townland.
		1897.				
Assistant Commissioners—	635	April 7,	Michael Devine, ...	Robert J. M'Geough, ...	Armagh, ...	Carran, ...
J. H. Ernst (Legal). J. H. M'Cormick. S. S. Swan.	629	„	Patrick Toner, ...	do.	do. ...	do. ...
	377	„	Patrick M'Cann, ...	do.	do. ...	Lislea, ...
	419	„	Michael M'Kee, ...	do.	do. ...	Sugaloe, ...
	363	„	Patrick Devlin, ...	Miss Emily G. Miller and anor., Reps. of Barbara Ogilvey.	do. ...	Tullymore Ag-wm.
	259	„	Graham Allen, ...	William J. Brown, ...	do. ...	Ballyrapple, ...
	236	„	Mary A. Boyd, Admix. of Nathaniel Boyd.	A. J. Little, ...	do. ...	Dunlargan, ...
	259	„	Robert Waddle, ...	do.	do. ...	do. ...
	327	„	James Adams, ...	do.	do. ...	do. ...
	376	„	Patrick Mallon, ...	Henry B. Armstrong, ...	do. ...	Lisbanly, ...
	313	„	John Mallon, ...	do.	do. ...	Dungory, ...
	226	„	William Loughran (Pat).	do.	do. ...	Corrickboy, ...
	315	„	Thomas Courtney,	Edward W. Verner, ...	do. ...	Hough, ...
	203	„	George Gibson, ...	Col. Inyr Burgess, ...	do. ...	Ballyworkid,
	304	„	Alexander M'Cutcheon.	John H. Parnell, ...	do. ...	Lisbanly, ...
	305	„	Do. ...	do.	do. ...	Kinnego, ...
	295	„	John Boggett, ...	do.	do. ...	Anglecaly, ...
	314	„	John Preney, ...	Rev. E. C. Hardy, ...	do. ...	Chroaggin, ...
	309	„	Henry Williamson,	Rev. W. J. Lattie, ...	do. ...	Keyrodam, ...
	339	„	Robert Wilson, ...	R. M'C. B. Skelton, ...	do. ...	Edenbury, ...
	254	„	Edward Largey, Ad. Admor. of James Largey.	Capt. W. H. Stroud, ...	do. ...	Ballinahone-more.
	167	„	Walter Ferris, ...	do.	do. ...	do. ...
	194	„	Christopher Hampton.	do.	do ...	do. ...
	253	„	Hugh Sherry, ...	Lieut.-Gen. Wm. Hardy, C.B.	do. ...	Tullywarpin, ...
	184	„	William M'Kenna,	Miss Agnes Kidd, ...	do. ...	Killyrurry, ...
	204	April 1,	Patrick Carr, ...	Arthur Benson, ...	do. ...	Tullasagh, ...
	225		John Carr, ...	do.	do. ...	do. ...
	227	„	Thomas Renter, ...	do.	do. ...	do. ...
	279	„	William J. M'Bride,	do.	do. ...	do. ...
	231	„	Terence Haughey,	do.	do. ...	do. ...
	311	„	Elizabeth Delaney,	Edward Quinn, ...	do. ...	Largyvale, ...
	230	„	Philip Lavery, ...	do.	do. ...	do. ...
	310	„	Elizabeth Delaney,	do.	do. ...	do. ...

SECOND STATUTORY TERM.

ARMAGH—*continued*.

Extent of Holding, Statute.	Poor Law Valuation.	Rent of Holding prior to creation of First Statutory Term.	Judicial Rent for First Statutory Term.	Judicial Rent for Second Statutory Term.	Record No. First Statutory Term.	Observations.
a. r. p.	£ s. d.	£ s. d.	£ s. d.	£ s. d.		
16 0 20	6 0 0	5 10 0	3 10 0	3 0 5	1638	
20 0 21	5 0 0	7 15 0	5 0 0	2 18 5	4823	
13 2 7	12 5 0	13 5 6	10 0 0	7 1 8	1036	
13 0 23	10 0 0	10 11 8	5 0 0	4 7 5	2877	
4 0 37	4 5 0	4 16 6	4 13 6	3 19 0	2701	
6 1 16	7 10 0	10 0 0	7 17 6	4 7 0	4475	
4 2 0	unascertained	9 0 0	5 13 0	4 3 8	1086	
8 0 20	3 10 0	9 0 0	5 0 0	2 7 6	1664	
5 0 30	5 15 0	14 10 0	7 0 0	4 11 0	1663	
16 1 4	16 10 0	16 7 6	13 13 0	5 5 6	84	
9 2 25	12 5 0	13 10 0	9 10 0	6 15 6	2584	
8 0 10	8 16 0	8 8 7	6 7 6	6 16 0	2825	
8 3 28	8 0 0	4 4 7	3 10 0	3 8 0	37	
23 3 10	24 15 0	24 16 0	20 0 0	14 0 0	3976	
6 0 26	6 5 0	8 2 0	4 5 0	3 10 0	2167	
6 1 22	6 15 0	7 10 0	4 0 0	3 6 0	2148	
30 0 20	27 10 0	26 16 0	23 10 0	18 7 0	2671	
2 1 10	3 10 0	4 12 0	3 16 0	1 10 7	266	
11 3 30	15 0 0	16 13 6	18 0 0	12 2 0	2480	
12 1 4	14 10 0	14 6 0	10 7 6	6 5 0	1565	
9 1 8	15 15 0	14 10 0	10 0 0	7 5 0	878	
56 0 20	45 0 0	48 19 7	38 0 0	29 7 6	874	
16 0 10	23 0 0	25 5 6	17 10 0	13 9 8	879	
71 1 26	84 0 0	87 6 3	80 0 0	18 0 0	1426	
6 0 8	4 15 0	8 4 6	6 0 0	3 1 0	1900	
16 3 20	17 5 0	16 18 6	14 10 0	8 11 6	4077	
14 0 0	10 10 0		10 6 6	6 8 6		
15 3 0	16 15 0	80 0 0	18 7 0	9 6 0	4061	This holding has been sub-divided since creation of 1st Statutory Term.
47 2 24	63 10 0		39 12 6	30 16 0		
24 0 5	23 5 0	24 10 0	20 0 0	11 16 8	4078	
6 3 20	13 10 0	17 3 6	13 5 0	9 0 0	1324	
70 0 35	64 10 0	64 3 2	50 0 0	34 8 4	1817	
9 0 30	17 10 0	28 10 0	15 15 0	10 16 4	1523	

ARMAGH—continued.

Extent of Holding Statute.	Poor Law Valuation.	Rent of Holding prior to ... of First Statutory Term.	Judicial Rent for First Statutory Term.	Judicial Rent for Second Statutory Term.	Record No. First Statutory Term.	Observations.
A. R. P.	£ s. d.	£ s. d.	£ s. d.	£ s. d.		
25 2 4	unascertained	55 5 6	62 0 0	52 5 0	1833	
6 1 10	9 10 0	5 17 10	2 15 0	1 6 9	57	
25 0 15	19 15 0	27 11 0	17 10 0	9 4 0	65	
10 0 20	20 0 0	11 9 10	7 10 0	6 1 0	1456	
6 2 10	10 10 0	6 9 8	7 8 0	6 5 6	844	
11 2 10	unascertained	14 15 9	9 10 0	6 15 0	1593	
18 3 0	14 5 0	17 7 9	11 0 0	7 13 8	4053	
9 0 20	15 15 0	12 8 9	9 10 0	7 5 0	5537	
63 3 30	41 10 0	61 3 10	27 10 0	18 10 0	877	
25 2 3	24 10 0	33 18 9	24 0 0	14 5 0	1744	
11 3 10	9 10 0	10 4 2	9 0 0	5 8 6	1756	
20 3 15	17 5 0	20 0 0	12 10 0	11 16 6	1768	
16 1 30	13 10 0	18 10 0	14 0 0	9 10 6	1767	
25 2 35	18 10 0	34 17 1	15 12 6	10 8 6	1769	
14 0 0	11 15 0	14 1 10	9 18 6	7 4 8	1770	
16 0 12	10 0 0	12 3 4	6 17 6	5 18 6	1771	
12 0 30	9 14 0	12 8 9	8 10 0	5 14 0	1789	
15 1 26	12 0 0	12 8 10	9 12 6	7 12 3	1780	
18 3 6	15 10 0	18 15 1	10 15 0	6 3 6	1778	
8 1 10	8 0 0	10 10 0	7 0 0	4 17 0	1782	
15 0 30	14 0 0	16 6 0	12 0 0	8 8 6	1776	
30 0 25	15 13 0	23 10 9	18 10 0	10 19 0	1779	
15 3 30	10 10 0	24 6 10	9 0 0	5 13 0	1784	
23 0 25	17 5 0	25 8 8	13 8 0	10 11 6	1787	
14 2 5	12 0 0	17 5 5	11 10 0	8 14 8	1780	
9 8 0	7 0 0	9 11 7	6 7 5	5 1 0	1783	
11 1 6	13 0 0	18 11 8	8 0 0	7 4 6	1785	
9 1 25	8 15 0	10 13 1	7 10 0	4 19 0	1258	
21 1 30	16 0 0	23 16 3	15 10 0	11 5 5	1756	
10 1 35	9 5 0	9 19 10	6 10 6	1 8 0	1760	
20 2 0	18 10 0	21 1 4	15 10 0	9 18 0	1763	
15 0 25	9 10 0	12 7 3	6 15 6	4 17 0	1765	
6 2 0	10 10 0	10 10 0	8 5 0	5 11 0	1831	

SECOND STATUTORY TERM.

COUNTY OF

Names of Assistant Commissioners by whom Cases were decided.	Record Number.	Date of Order.	Name of Tenant.	Name of Landlord.	Poor Law Union.	Townland.
		1897.				
Assistant Commissioners— J. H. Rowe (Legal). J. H. M'Cormack. R. S. Doran.	[illegible]	April 1,	Robert Farrell, ...	Cecilia F. Cope & others, Committee of Estate of F. R. Cope.	Armagh, ...	E.[illegible], ...
	[illegible]	"	William Wilson and another.	do. ...	do. ...	do. ...
	[illegible]	"	William Gilmour, ...	do. ...	do. ...	do. ...
	[illegible]	"	William M'Cune & another.	do. ...	do. ...	do. ...
	[illegible]	"	Robert Parr, ...	do. ...	do. ...	do. ...
	[illegible]	"	Thomas Thompson,	do. ...	do. ...	do. ...
	[illegible]	"	John Gibson, ...	do. ...	do. ...	do. ...
	[illegible]	"	Samuel Parr, ...	do. ...	do. ...	do. ...
	[illegible]	"	James [illegible], ...	do.	do. ...	do. ...
	[illegible]	"	William Wilson and another.	do.	do. ...	[illegible],
	[illegible]	"	Elizabeth Douglas,	do.	do. ...	E.[illegible], ...
W. F. Bailey (Legal). A. Kendall. J. Mackenzie.	[illegible]	Apr. 14,	Mary Anne Cumberton.	Rev. George D. M'Clure,	Lurgan, ...	[illegible], ...
J. H. Rowe (Legal). M. S. Fetherston. J. G. S. MacNeill.	[illegible]	Apr. 12,	Jas. Thompson, Exor. of Mary Thompson.	William Reed, ...	Castleblayney,	Tullyvallen, ...
	[illegible]	"	Thomas Longtreen, Admor. of Patrick Longtreen.	Francis E. [illegible], ...	do. ...	[illegible], ...
						Total, ...

COUNTY OF

Names of Assistant Commissioners by whom Cases were decided.	Record Number.	Date of Order.	Name of Tenant.	Name of Landlord.	Poor Law Union.	Townland.
Assistant Commissioners— J. H. Rowe (Legal). F. O'Callaghan. L. Coffey.	[illegible]	April 7,	Michael Cassidy, ...	Major H. E. Maxwell, ...	Cavan, ...	[illegible] ...
	[illegible]	"	Patrick Galligan, ...	do.	do. ...	[illegible], ...
	[illegible]	"	Nicholas Cassidy,	do.	do. ...	do. ...
	[illegible]	"	John Keegan, ...	do.	do. ...	[illegible] ...
	[illegible]	"	James Fitzsd, ...	do.	do. ...	do. ...
	[illegible]	"	Patrick Gaffney, ...	do.	do. ...	Lavagh ...
	[illegible]	"	James Harvin, ...	do.	do. ...	do. ...
	[illegible]	"	Thomas Smith, ...	Lewis Buchanan, ...	do. ...	[illegible], ...
	[illegible]	"	Thomas Dobson, ...	do.	do. ...	do. ...
	[illegible]	"	Martin Reddan, ...	Major R. W. Fleming, ...	do. ...	[illegible], ...

SECOND STATUTORY TERM.

ARMAGH—*continued.*

Extent of Holding, Statute.	Poor Law Valuation.	Rent of Holding prior to execution of First Statutory Term.	Judicial Rent for First Statutory Term.	Judicial Rent for Second Statutory Term.	Record No. First Statutory Term.	Observations.
A. R. P.	£ s. d.	£ s. d.	£ s. d.	£ s. d.		
9 0 15	5 15 0	5 13 4	2 8 0	1 12 0	1867	
60 1 19	45 18 0	40 17 6	34 0 0	[illegible] 4 5	1857	
5 0 0	4 5 0	6 19 5	6 15 0	3 12 5	[illegible]	
63 2 36	61 5 0	61 0 0	44 0 0	37 15 6	1853	
13 0 0	15 5 0	15 1 6	11 10 0	7 19 0	1581	
15 0 20	17 15 0	17 16 9	15 0 0	7 18 0	1530	
18 1 [illegible]	18 10 0	18 11 10	16 0 0	9 15 0	[illegible]	
7 3 15	9 0 0	9 17 0	8 0 0	5 6 5	1594	
9 3 31	10 10 0	9 17 6	9 0 0	8 12 6	1594	
6 3 11	7 5 0	7 0 0	5 15 0	4 5 0	1848	
70 1 30	34 15 0	34 7 6	27 0 0	17 15 0	1818	
9 1 0	16 10 0	27 10 0	23 10 0	15 2 6	[illegible]	
[illegible] 2 18	14 15 0	18 4 2	18 10 0	10 0 6	393	
[illegible] 1 10	18 1 0	19 11 3	11 0 0	8 10 0	387	
1,675 1 [illegible]	1,[illegible] 10 0	1,[illegible] 17 0½	1,1[illegible] 0 10	808 1 4		

CAVAN.

SECOND STATUTORY TERM.

COUNTY OF

Names of Assistant Commissioners by whom Cases were decided.	Record Number.	Date of Order.	Name of Tenant.	Name of Landlord.	Poor Law Union.	Townland.
Assistant Commissioners –		1887.				
J. H. Knox (Legal). F. O'C[illegible]. L. Carey.	165	Mar. 11,	Thomas Sheridan,	Matthew W. Webb, ...	Cavan, ...	Ballygrave, ...
	159	April 7,	John M'Mahon, ...	Major S. W. Fleming,	do. ...	Garrymore, ...
	201	"	Andrew Smith, ...	do.	do. ...	Garrymore and commons,
	162	"	John Griffith, ...	Rev. T. G. J. Phillips, ...	do. ...	Carrowkeelaghan,
	164	"	John Duncan, ...	do.	do. ...	do. ...
	163	"	Michael Brady, ...	do.	do. ...	Mullaghmore,
	166	"	William Best, ...	do.	do. ...	do. ...
	177	"	Francis Best, ...	do.	do. ...	do. ...
	165	"	John Sheridan, ...	do.	do. ...	Drughill, ...
	160	"	John Pearson, ...	do.	do. ...	do. ...
	176	"	William Best, ...	do.	do. ...	do. ...
	167	"	John Griffith, ...	do.	do. ...	Drughillaun,
	169	"	James Sheridan, ...	do.	do. ...	Tirgorraly, ...
	170	"	Do. ...	do.	do. ...	do. ...
	171	"	Do. ...	do.	do. ...	do. ...
	173	"	Mary Sheridan, ...	do.	do. ...	do. ...
	179	"	Robert M'Adams,	do.	do. ...	Carrowkeelaghan.
	182	"	Patrick Lee, ...	Major W. G. Smith, ...	do. ...	Carragh, ...
	187	"	Young Pratt, ...	Messrs Brooke & ors.,	do. ...	Tonymore, ...
	188	"	Margaret Smith, ...	do	do. ...	do. ...
	189	"	John Smith, ...	do.	do. ...	do. ...
	180	"	Robert Pratt, ...	do.	do. ...	do. ...
	66	"	Lawrence Reilly, ...	Mrs Susan Johnston, ...	do. ...	Rossnagun, ...
	147	"	Michael Gaffney, ...	T. C. Burrowes, ...	do. ...	Aughnaval, ...
	174	"	Margery Cassidy & Bernard Kearns	Rev. T. G. J. Phillips, ...	do. ...	Carrowkeelaghan & mill Tonel, ...

SECOND STATUTORY TERM.

CAVAN—continued.

Extent of Holding. Statute.	Poor Law Valuation.	Rent of Holding prior to creation of First Statutory Term.	Judicial Rent for First Statutory Term.	Judicial Rent for Second Statutory Term.	Record No., First Statutory Term.	Observations.
A. R. P.	£ s. d.	£ s. d.	£ s. d.	£ s. d.		
21 1 6	12 15 0	10 5 0	14 0 0	11 5 0	33 Agt.	By consent.
7 1 5	4 16 0	6 10 0	5 10 0	3 16 0	259 c. n.	
17 0 23	19 10 0	13 15 0	11 5 0	10 10 0	591 c. n.	
13 2 31	6 15 0	12 3 6½	9 16 8	5 6 0	410 Agt.	
27 1 26	21 5 0	15 18 8	17 16 8	15 0 0	1112 Agt.	
31 3 16	20 15 0	22 15 9	18 11 4	13 3 8	239 Agt.	
20 0 18	18 5 0	15 9 8	13 19 8	8 8 0	244 Agt.	
23 0 33	16 0 0	18 18 8	13 18 10	9 5 0	240 Agt.	
30 0 5	21 10 0	28 13 3	19 18 0	14 15 0	241 Agt.	
31 1 7	23 5 0	23 0 1	20 5 0	15 11 0	780 Agt.	
30 1 0	18 10 0	19 0 1	14 10 0	10 0 0	779 Agt.	
27 3 13	11 5 0	21 18 0	17 16 4	13 0 0	609 Agt.	
20 3 20	13 0 0	16 13 0	11 10 0	9 0 0	781 Agt.	
46 3 1	28 10 0	37 3 3	29 0 6	23 10 0	246 Agt.	
13 2 0	6 0 0	11 8 8	8 18 6	6 15 0	249 Agt.	
19 1 20	12 10 0	14 8 8	11 5 1	9 16 0	243 Agt.	
17 0 0	10 0 0	10 13 8	9 1 5	6 15 0	203 Agt.	
18 3 33	10 18 0	12 4 6	10 15 0	9 5 0	1671 Agt.	
79 1 34	67 5 0	70 0 0	64 0 0	54 0 0	697	
84 0 15	unvalued	60 0 0	60 0 0	53 10 0	400	
46 0 25	56 10 0	65 0 0	40 0 0	33 0 0	[illegible]	
43 3 19	26 10 0	30 16 0	30 16 0	23 10 0	[illegible]	
16 3 13	14 15 0	21 10 0	15 10 0	14 0 0	53 c. n.	
20 3 16	9 7 6	11 10 0	9 0 0	8 0 0	387 c. n.	
30 0 21	40 15 0	60 3 1	35 19 1	28 18 0	778 Agt.	
786 0 9	503 5 6	610 11 6½	542 1 8	413 10 0		

DONEGAL.

SECOND STATUTORY TERM.

COUNTY OF

Names of Assistant Commissioners by whom Cases were decided.	Record Number.	Date of Order.	Name of Tenant.	Name of Landlord.	Poor Law Union.	Townland.
Assistant Commissioners—		1887.				
	616	Apr. 23,	Connell O'Donnell,	Earl of Arran, ...	Donegal, ...	Clogher, ...
G. H. Turner (Legal). R. H. Ferguson. J. A. Rynd.	620	"	James [illegible], ...	do.	do. ...	Calliaghy, ...
	619	"	Hugh Cassidy, senr., Admr. of John Cassidy, deceased.	do.	do. ...	Claggan, ...
	627	"	Michael Dunnion,	do.	do. ...	Calliaghy, ...
	628	"	Anne Hamilton, Admx. of Robert Hamilton, decd.	do.	do. ...	Carvan, ...
	630	"	James M'Garry, ...	do.	do. ...	Birch-hill, ...
	631	"	Charles Callaghan,	do.	do. ...	do. ...
	618	"	John M'Girr, ...	do.	do. ...	Cloonrivinagun.
	615	"	James [illegible], ...	do.	do. ...	do. ...
	626	"	Anthony M'Ginty,	do.	do. ...	Birch-hill, ...
	621	"	James Cassidy, ...	do.	do. ...	Carvan, ...
	617	"	Francis Thompson, ...	do.	do. ...	Birch-hill, ...
	611	"	Babington Miller,	do.	do. ...	Clardrumnaron.
	613	"	John Cassidy, ...	do.	do. ...	Calliaghy, ...
	619	"	Thomas Kearney, ...	do.	do. ...	Clardrumagahan.
	[illegible]	"	Robert Love, ...	do.	do. ...	Fan-lane, ...
	39	"	Charles M'Loughlin,	Miss Mary C. E. Johnston,	Stranorlar, ...	Cronick, ...
	[illegible]	"	James Irwin, ...	do.	do. ...	Drumnaha, ...
	270	"	Charles Kee, ...	do.	do. ...	do. ...
	401	"	William Wilson, ...	do.	do. ...	do. ...
	[illegible]	"	Letitia Kee, ...	do.	do. ...	do. ...
	4	"	William Gallagher,	do.	do. ...	Cronick, ...
	[illegible]	"	Bernard Gallen, Rep. of Patrick Gallen.	do.	do. ...	Ballyarrell, ...
	[illegible]	"	James Harper, ...	Colonel F. Mansfield, ...	do. ...	Killygordon ...
D. Toohey (Legal). S. H. Miller. J. W. Barrett.	154	Mar. 9,	John F. Doherty, ...	William S. Harte, ...	Inishowen, ...	Ardagh, ...
	155	"	Margaret Hannon,	do.	do. ...	do. ...
	157	"	Ann Doherty, ...	do.	do. ...	do. ...
	147	"	Daniel Tolan, ...	do.	do. ...	do. ...
	159	"	William Doherty, ...	do.	do. ...	do. ...
	149	"	Catherine Doherty,	do.	do. ...	do. ...

SECOND STATUTORY TERM.

DONEGAL—*continued.*

Extent of Holding Statute.	Poor Law Valuation.	Rent of Holding prior to fixing of First Statutory Term.	Judicial Rent for First Statutory Term.	Judicial Rent for Second Statutory Term.	Record No. of Second Statutory T…
A. R. P.	£ s. d.	£ s. d.	£ s. d.	£ s. d.	
[illegible] 5 15	3 5 0	5 7 8	3 10 6	2 4 10	[illegible]
71 2 0	5 5 0	5 2 0	5 10 0	4 4 11	[illegible]
18 2 30	4 10 0	4 11 0	5 4 0	8 19 5	[illegible]
[illegible] 3 25	2 2 0	4 2 6	3 0 0	3 0 0	[illegible]
74 0 0	[illegible] 15 0	43 0 0	[illegible] 10 0	21 4 9	[illegible]
15 3 15	7 10 0	11 4 0	7 8 8	6 14 6	[illegible]
11 3 21	8 5 0	5 5 10	3 15 0	2 4 4	[illegible]
10 3 5	6 5 0	9 17 2	6 0 0	7 1 10	[illegible]
41 3 30	67 10 0	30 10 0	27 10 0	20 3 6	[illegible]
12 1 9	6 10 0	9 2 0	4 17 1	5 16 10	[illegible]
12 3 31	7 4 0	8 19 7	4 15 6	8 8 2	[illegible]
17 2 26	9 0 0	11 5 8	7 10 0	3 18 0	[illegible]
[illegible] 1 31	41 0 0	32 0 0	[illegible] 0 0	29 11 4	[illegible]
7 0 30	2 5 0	8 10 0	3 0 0	3 0 0	611
[illegible] 3 1	18 10 0	[illegible] 18 0	19 5 0	16 8 3	[illegible]
33 5 36	5 15 0	8 5 0	7 0 0	6 3 5	[illegible]
[illegible] 3 [illegible]	31 10 0	45 0 0	36 0 0	27 19 5	[illegible]
[illegible] 2 0	14 5 0	[illegible] 5 0	17 10 0	9 4 1	[illegible]
17 1 27	7 10 0	18 10 0	8 0 0	5 11 4	[illegible]
84 0 0	[illegible] 10 0	26 0 0	[illegible] 0 0	19 8 0	[illegible]
11 0 0	7 5 0	10 10 0	7 0 0	5 7 9	[illegible]
[illegible] 1 [illegible]	[illegible] 15 0	27 0 0	17 10 0	14 18 10	[illegible]
[illegible] 0 5	31 0 0	40 0 0	33 0 0	23 15 3	411
45 0 0	64 0 0	44 10 0	44 10 0	33 4 1	[illegible]
16 3 31	4 0 0	5 0 0	4 15 6	3 15 0	[illegible]
[illegible] 1 30	6 0 0	9 6 4	6 3 10	5 0 0	[illegible]
10 3 31	4 15 0	7 0 5	5 10 6	3 19 0	[illegible]

SECOND STATUTORY TERM.

COUNTY OF

Names of Assistant Commissioners by whom Cases were decided.	Record Number.	Date of Order.	Name of Tenant.	Name of Landlord.	Poor Law Union.	Townland.
Assistant Commissioners—		1897.				
G. H. Tenlow (Legal). G. N. Callwell. W. S. Henry.	19	Mar. 30,	Paul Gallagher, ...	Lucky Brown, ...	Scrabo, ...	Ballybrue, ...
	17	"	Wm. J. A. Wray,	James B. Daley, ...	do. ...	Douglas, ...
						Total, .

COUNTY OF

Names of Assistant Commissioners by whom Cases were decided.	Record Number.	Date of Order.	Name of Tenant.	Name of Landlord.	Poor Law Union.	Townland.
Assistant Commissioners— W. F. Bailey (Legal). W. Shaw. Ashley Kendall.	1307	April 14,	Robert M'Murray,	Mrs. Sarah E. Wray, ...	Lurgan, ...	Cargaway, ...
	1308	"	Richard Brown, ...	do.	do. ...	do. ...
	1309	"	Do. ...	do.	do. ...	do. ...
	1256	"	Catherine Black, ...	do.	do. ...	do. ...
	1184a	"	Jane Gillespie, ...	do.	do. ...	do. ...
	1165	"	John M'Murray, ...	do.	do. ...	do. ...
	1166	"	Richard Brown, ...	do.	do. ...	do. ...
	1690	"	James Adamson, ...	A. H. Riddle, ...	do. ...	Ballydougan, ...
	1683	"	John Brown, ...	do.	do. ...	do. ...
	1687	"	Catherine O'Neill, ...	do.	do. ...	do. ...
	1686	"	James M'Conville,	do.	do. ...	do. ...
	1695	"	Geo. Adamson, sen.,	do.	do. ...	do. ...
	1681	"	Valentine Livingstone,	do.	do. ...	do. ...
	1678	"	Elizabeth Pollock, ...	do.	do. ...	do. ...
	1675	"	Nicholas Dynes, ...	do.	do. ...	do. ...
	1674	"	Samuel Dale, ...	do.	do. ...	do. ...
	1673	"	John M'Conville, ...	do.	do. ...	do. ...
	1670	"	Samuel Dale, ...	do.	do. ...	do. ...
	1686	"	Alex. Chambers, ...	do.	do. ...	do. ...
	1667	"	James Chambers, ...	do.	do. ...	do. ...
	1671	"	George Wilson, ...	do.	do. ...	do. ...
	1669	"	George Adamson, ...	do.	do. ...	do. ...
	1676	"	Abraham Dynes, ...	do.	do. ...	do. ...
	1677	"	Robert Pollock, ...	do.	do. ...	do. ...
	1684	"	James M'Cormick,	do.	do. ...	do. ...
	1682	"	William [illegible],	do.	do. ...	do. ...
	1683	"	James M'Guigan,	do.	do. ...	do. ...
	1694	"	Margt. Moore & ors.,	do.	do. ...	do. ...

SECOND STATUTORY TERM.

DONEGAL—*continued.*

Extent of Holding. Statute Measure.	Poor Law Valuation.	Rent of Holding prior to granting of First Statutory Term.	Judicial Rent for First Statutory Term.	Judicial Rent for Second Statutory Term.	Record No. First Statutory Term.	Observations.
A. R. P.	£ s. d.	£ s. d.	£ s. d.	£ s. d.		
17 3 32	5 0 0	8 0 0	5 10 0	5 10 0	610	
15 0 25	11 0 0	10 10 0	7 0 0	6 0 0	15	
1,067 3 13	460 16 0	623 1 11	483 17 11	346 19 3		

DOWN.

Extent of Holding. Statute Measure.	Poor Law Valuation.	Rent of Holding prior to granting of First Statutory Term.	Judicial Rent for First Statutory Term.	Judicial Rent for Second Statutory Term.	Record No. First Statutory Term.	Observations.
8 1 0	11 0 0	10 4 0	8 3 0	6 4 0	658	
4 1 37	unascertained.	5 4 0	3 15 0	2 19 0	1083	
10 1 18	10 15 0	12 8 0	9 18 5	7 5 0	631	
4 0 35	7 10 0	7 10 2	5 10 0	3 8 0	1080	
25 2 5	31 0 0	31 5 0	25 0 0	17 14 0	693	
26 1 20	37 0 0	20 0 0	24 0 0	16 10 0	615	
21 1 25	15 10 0	18 5 3	12 4 8	8 14 0	430	
4 0 32	5 0 0	4 17 4	4 5 0	3 3 5	8782	
14 1 5	24 0 0	16 10 10	15 5 0	10 9 0	2257	
12 2 0	14 0 0	16 5 0	11 15 0	7 15 0	5870	
9 0 35	3 5 0	4 16 4	5 2 6	1 13 0	3073	
4 0 35	5 14 0	4 17 4	4 5 0	6 0 0	2293	
18 3 0	17 0 0	16 18 4	13 0 0	8 15 0	3013	
10 0 16	15 5 0	11 4 0	8 0 0	6 0 0	2020	
18 3 30	15 5 0	24 15 9	18 10 0	9 5 0	2259	
35 0 27	47 0 0	50 15 10	27 0 0	21 18 0	2234	
2 3 10	3 10 0	4 15 4	3 3 8	1 15 0	3673	
7 1 32	10 10 0	5 3 6	7 5 0	5 16 5	7294	
18 0 38	15 0 0	24 15 4	13 0 0	9 10 0	3288	
20 1 35	15 0 0	21 7 6	10 8 8	8 17 4	3014	
35 0 0	49 15 0	43 0 0	37 0 0	29 0 0	3016	
15 2 30	25 5 0	20 5 0	18 10 0	15 0 0	7294	
41 0 25	48 15 0	44 11 0	36 0 0	28 18 0	2330	
11 0 35	18 5 0	11 14 4	8 0 0	5 16 5	2018	
5 0 0	8 15 0	9 15 5	7 16 0	5 16 0	1893	
30 3 10	42 15 0	24 14 11	23 5 0	23 18 0	2290	
8 0 18	8 5 0	9 5 10	2 3 10	1 18 0	2327	
4 2 5	7 0 0	6 9 11	3 5 0	2 17 0	2293	

SECOND STATUTORY TERM.

DOWN—*continued.*

Extent of Holding (Statute).	Poor Law Valuation.	Rent of Holding prior to fixing of First Statutory Term.	Judicial Rent for First Statutory Term.	Judicial Rent for Second Statutory Term.	Record No. First Statutory Term.	Observations.
A. R. P.	£ s. d.	£ s. d.	£ s. d.	£ s. d.		
30 0 13	[illegible] 0 0	[illegible] 13 10	25 10 0	19 4 0	2497	
13 1 5	24 0 0	21 6 6	16 0 0	15 10 0	2323	
24 0 [illegible]	43 15 0	37 9 8	24 5 0	[illegible] 0 0	[illegible]19	
7 0 0	10 0 0	7 0 0	4 10 4	5 6 0	2321	
5 2 [illegible]	6 0 0	6 6 0	5 0 0	4 15 0	2405	
12 2 8	20 5 0	15 10 4	11 10 0	8 9 0	2405	
9 3 [illegible]	7 10 0	8 0 8	5 0 0	3 13 6	2375	
6 0 33	5 15 0	6 8 0	6 10 0	1 6 6	2406	
6 1 10	8 5 0	8 5 8	6 0 0	2 17 6	2317	
5 1 15	4 10 0	5 12 8	3 5 6	3 10 0	2327	
6 5 10	8 15 5	7 11 8	4 5 4	5 13 0	3-[illegible]	
15 0 12	15 0 0	24 10 0	14 0 0	11 10 0	810	By consent.
13 1 25	17 0 0	20 0 0	15 0 0	11 0 0	1003	
[illegible] 0 20	28 10 0	37 5 3	23 0 0	14 5 0	1879	
[illegible] 1 30	24 5 0	28 4 7	21 0 0	12 15 0	1878	
6 3 20	7 10 0	7 10 0	6 10 0	4 10 0	1887	
4 0 30	5 0 0	4 18 0	4 0 0	3 0 0	1876	
23 0 [illegible]	25 5 0	37 7 0	22 10 0	15 17 0	1085	
6 1 0	6 0 0	8 17 11	6 12 5	6 0 0	1086	
6 1 [illegible]	7 0 0	9 15 7	7 0 0	4 10 0	1085	
16 1 20	18 10 0	24 0 5	17 15 0	11 5 0	1084	
10 0 30	15 6 0	10 1 4	12 0 0	7 10 0	1085	
[illegible] 0 15	39 15 0	53 2 0	[illegible] 0 0	19 10 0	1051	
42 1 [illegible]	50 5 0	50 13 0	45 0 0	[illegible] 0 0	2425	
[illegible] 1 0	37 0 0	40 0 0	35 0 0	30 10 0	1874	
16 1 [illegible]	10 10 0	18 3 0	15 0 6	7 10 0	0725	
11 0 25	14 10 0	—	12 0 0	9 13 6	176	Holding altered since creation of First Statutory Term.
65 0 10	56 5 0	47 3 8	53 0 0	[illegible] 15 0	176	

SECOND STATUTORY TERM.

COUNTY OF

Names of Assistant Commissioners by whom Cases were decided.	Record Number.	Date of Order.	Name of Tenant.	Name of Landlord.	Poor Law Union.	Townland.
Assistant Commissioners—		1877.				
W. F. Bailey (Legal). S. Byrne. S. G. Williams.	916	April 14,	Thomas Donaldson,	Alexander H. Gordon ...	Newtownards,	Ballyhenry,
	917	"	Isaac Moorhead, ...	do. ...	do. ...	Drumree, ...
	918	"	Hugh Coulter, ...	do.	do. ...	Ballyhenry,
	919	"	Eleanor M'Kee, Admix. of Robert M'Kee,	do.	do. ...	do. ...
	762	"	James M'Cauley, ...	William Gibson, ...	do. ...	Craigboy, ...
	763	"	William Byers, ...	Lord Dunleath, ...	do. ...	Ballyholey, ...
	1294	"	Samuel Orr, ...	Genl. Wm. Mussenden,	do. ...	Ballygowan, ...
	1017	"	Ellen Brown, ...	Genl. W. R. Montgomery,	do. ...	Ballymurphy,
	1014	"	Alexander Wright,	do.	do. ...	do. ...
	1010	"	John Gilmour, ...	do.	do. ...	Ballygarvie, ...
	1016	"	Peter Davidson, ...	do.	do. ...	Ballymurphy,
	1253	"	John Jamison, ...	Marquis of Dufferin and Ava,	do. ...	Ballyrushbeagh Major,
	600	"	Robert Jamison, ...	Adam M'Nally, ...	do. ...	do. ...
	603	"	Mrs. Mary Huddleston,	Baron Trevor, ...	do. ...	Monlough, ...
	605	"	James Blair, ...	do.	do. ...	Mountyon, ...
	604	"	Margt. J. Huddleston,	do.	do. ...	do. ...
	606	"	Samuel M'K. Turbitt,	do.	do. ...	do. ...
	609	"	Robert Knight, ...	do.	do. ...	Monlough, ...
	614	"	Thomas Kenny, ...	James Craig, ...	do. ...	Ballyclaverty, ...
	613	"	James Stewart, ...	do.	do. ...	do. ...
	619	"	Alexander H. Johnston,	do.	do. ...	do. ...
	1089	"	Jane Adams, ...	do.	do. ...	Ballyrainey, ...
	334	"	Margaret Smyth, ...	do.	do. ...	do. ...
	1257	"	James Copeland, ...	do.	do. ...	do. ...
	1116	"	Jane Adams, ...	do.	do. ...	do. ...
	1240	"	Samuel Glover, ...	W. R. M'Connell, ...	do. ...	Ballydoonan,
	1241	"	John Anderson, ...	do.	do. ...	do. ...
	1304	"	Thomas Cavanagh, ...	do.	do. ...	do. ...
	1235	"	Wm. Montgomery,	do.	do. ...	Tullykildare,
	1165	"	Robert Reid, ...	do.	do. ...	Ballydoonan,
						Total, ...

0	[illegible]	
0	1870	
0	1878	
0	781	
0	1878	
0	2377	
0	[illegible]	
0	[illegible]	
0	[illegible]	
0	[illegible]	
0	[illegible]	
0	[illegible]	
0	[illegible]	
0	[illegible]	
0	[illegible]	
0	[illegible]	
0	[illegible]	
0	[illegible]	
0	2819	
0	[illegible]	
0 0	8716	Holding divided since First Statutory Term created.
0	8780	
0	1880	

Names of Assistant Commissioners by whom Cases were decided.	Record Number.	Date of Order.	Name of Tenant.	Name of Landlord.	Poor Law Union.	Townland.
Assistant Commissioners—		1897.				
J. H. Rolls (Legal). G. A. G. Anderson. W. Jeffcott.	185	Apr. 8,	William Maguire,	Miss F. C. Armstrong, ...	Clogher, ...	Kilrud, ...
	186	"	Samuel Coulson, ...	Earl of Erne, ...	do. ...	Belmount and another,
	187	"	Do., ...	do.	do. ...	Clonmaulsy, ...
	185	"	John Nixon, ...	do.	do. ...	Gortgarvan, ...
	180	"	William Irwin, ...	Mrs J. Auchinleck, ...	do. ...	Shaunesh Oran,
	187	"	Thomas Kearns, ...	Miss Maude Hamilton, ...	do. ...	Aghnafoggers,
	189	"	James Dempsey, ...	do.	do. ...	Curraleighy, ...
	209	"	Michael Boggan, ...	William H. Haire, ...	do. ...	Coolesmills, ...
	188	"	Bernard Carey, ...	Miss Maude Hamilton,	do. ...	Curraleighy, ...
	190	"	William M'Mahon, Lid. Admr. of Hugh M'Caffrey, deceased.	do.	do. ...	do. ...
	135	"	John William Kells,	Rev. Henry Sweeny, ...	do. ...	McElyouggerrad,
	185	"	Samuel Coulson, ...	Earl of Erne, ...	do. ...	Belmount, ...
C. H. Teeling (Legal). A. R. Montgomery. R. W. Gamble.	374	Apr. 10,	Patrick Cassidy, (Brown).	Eliza Ferguson, ...	Enniskillen,	Glengesh, ...
C. H. Teeling (Legal). H. Jennings. G. M'Elderry.	397	Apr. 23,	James Martin, ...	Henry M. Campbell and another.	Irvinestown,	Ballaghmore,
	697	Mar. 23,	James M'Mahon, ...	Thomas Porter and other,	Lisnaskea, ...	Drumsirry, ...
	679	Mar. 24,	William Finlay, ...	Colonel J. D. Johnston,	do. ...	Millwood, ...
						Total, ...

SECOND STATUTORY TERM.

FERMANAGH.

Extent of Holding Statute.			Poor Law Valuation.			Rent of Holding prior to First Statutory Term.			Judicial Rent for First Statutory Term.			Judicial Rent for Second Statutory Term.			Record No. First Statutory Term.	Observations.
A.	R.	P.	£	s.	d.	£	s.	d.	£	s.	d.	£	s.	d.		
21	1	35	17	15	0	17	5	0	15	0	0	10	0	0	1097	
38	0	0	31	15	0	37	1	4	[illegible]	0	0	18	5	0	[illegible]	
[illegible]	1	[illegible]	[illegible]	10	0	19	7	0	14	7	0	12	12	0	[illegible]	
10	0	[illegible]	18	15	0	14	3	10	13	10	0	8	[illegible]	0	1645	
19	1	10	17	0	0	19	0	0	16	0	0	11	10	0	[illegible]	
10	3	[illegible]	7	5	0	7	5	0	6	0	0	5	17	0	[illegible]	
13	2	5	9	15	0	9	15	0	7	15	0	5	18	0	1097	
[illegible]	1	[illegible]	7	10	0	11	3	4	10	10	0	7	17	0	[illegible]	
6	[illegible]	[illegible]	5	15	0	5	15	0	4	15	0	[illegible]	[illegible]	0	[illegible]	
24	1	[illegible]	17	10	0	17	10	0	15	10	0	10	16	0	[illegible]	
[illegible]	1	35	[illegible]	0	0	25	0	0	[illegible]	0	0	14	17	0	581	
45	[illegible]	18	84	5	0	40	0	0	[illegible]	10	0	[illegible]	16	0	1547	
[illegible]	4	[illegible]	13	10	0	[illegible]	0	0	14	10	0	11	3	0	1576	
41	0	[illegible]	24	10	0	[illegible]	0	0	[illegible]	0	0	17	0	0	[illegible] Agt.	
6	2	15	1	15	0	2	10	0	7	0	0	1	12	0	[illegible] Agt.	By consent.
10	[illegible]	[illegible]	7	5	0	12	0	0	10	10	0	7	0	0	2176 Agt.	do.
[illegible]	1	24	[illegible]	15	0	[illegible]	15	5	[illegible]	12	0	167	0	0		

LONDONDERRY.

IRISH LAND COMMISSION.

SECOND STATUTORY TERM.

Date of Order.	Name of Tenant.	Name of Landlord.
1897		
Mar. [illegible]	John Stewart, junr.,	Hon. [illegible] Cumming.
,,	Archibald M'Neill,	Viscount Montgomery [illegible]
,,	George M'Neill, ...	do. ...
,,	William Ramage, ...	T. R. B. Cope and ot[illegible] Trustees of T. R. B[illegible] deceased.
,,	Andrew M'Lurg[illegible],	Robert Given,
,,	William Archibald,	do. ...
,,	John M'Pherson, ...	Mrs. R. Torrens & [illegible]
,,	Patrick M'Cahan,	do. ...
,,	John M'Pherson, ...	do. ...

SECOND STATUTORY TERM.

LONDONDERRY—*continued*.

Extent of Holding, Statute.	Poor Law Valuation.	Rent of Holding prior to operation of First Statutory Term.	Judicial Rent for First Statutory Term.	Judicial Rent for Second Statutory Term.	Record No. First Statutory Term.	Observations.
A. R. P.	£ s. d.	£ s. d.	£ s. d.	£ s. d.		
35 1 37	18 10 0	16 10 0	12 0 0	9 15 0	1001	
84 3 0	57 0 0	66 13 4	66 0 0	48 17 6	578	
38 2 25	33 5 0	33 6 8	27 0 0	22 1 0	377	
43 3 6	61 0 0	38 9 9	33 10 0	34 2 0	1546	
38 1 12	19 0 0	30 0 0	23 0 0	17 14 0	2164	
19 3 30	12 0 0	19 0 0	14 10 0	14 10 0	2367	
35 0 27	5 10 0	11 11 1	5 0 0	5 8 0	1569	
40 3 25	17 10 0	20 9 7½	15 0 0	14 0 0	1634	
22 2 35	14 0 5	67 0 0	14 0 0	43 15 0	1940	
28 2 34	13 5 0	15 7 7	13 0 0	11 10 0	1561	
13 0 27	4 10 0	5 13 9	5 0 0	4 0 0	1486	
35 1 16	19 5 0	27 18 4	14 0 0	11 7 6	1546	
46 3 0	16 5 0	17 18 1	16 10 0	14 17 0	1608	
780 0 14	403 5 4	604 18 4½	508 17 0	423 15 4		

MONAGHAN.

Extent of Holding, Statute.	Poor Law Valuation.	Rent of Holding prior to operation of First Statutory Term.	Judicial Rent for First Statutory Term.	Judicial Rent for Second Statutory Term.	Record No. First Statutory Term.	Observations.
63 0 6	38 5 0	34 11 8	25 0 0	18 17 9	116	
38 3 22	unascertained	21 5 1	11 14 0	11 2 0	183	
41 1 0	16 16 0	24 16 0	18 0 0	15 16 9	49	
18 3 30	38 0 0	33 9 1	16 0 0	11 16 1	56	
18 3 18	5 14 0	6 14 4	6 10 0	4 13 5	703	
10 1 5	6 0 0	6 16 10	5 0 0	4 17 6	703	
20 1 30	14 0 0	20 1 1	18 10 0	11 16 8	759	
36 1 10	40 0 0	37 3 1	30 10 0	26 15 4	841	
14 2 0	9 5 0	9 15 5	8 10 0	5 18 3	73 Agt.	
6 1 20	3 15 0	4 13 5	3 10 0	2 7 9	73	
28 1 10	6 6 0	9 15 3	5 0 0	4 0 0	66	
11 0 0	4 15 0	6 6 10	3 10 0	3 5 10	68	
9 3 20	4 0 0	6 11 7	5 6 0	3 6 0	67	
10 1 36	4 10 0	5 18 10	3 10 0	3 4 9	68	
17 3 0	8 15 0	12 19 8	8 10 0	6 16 11	84	

SECOND STATUTORY TERM.

COUNTY OF

Names of Assistant Commissioners by whom Cases were decided.	Record Number.	Date of Order.	Name of Tenant.	Name of Landlord.	Poor Law Union.	Townland.
Assistant Commissioners—		1887.				
J. H. Ross (Legal). M. S. Patterson. J. S. S. Moffat.	325	Apr. 13,	Michael Lavelle, ...	Robert Brown & another, Trustees of A. R. Montgomery (a minor).	Castleblayney	Carrickatee, ...
	377	"	Do. ...	do.	do. ...	do. ...
	327	"	Eliza Lavelle, Ltd. Admix. of Laurence Lavelle.	do.	do. ...	do. ...
	333	"	Samuel Graham, ...	do.	do. ...	do. ...
	319	"	Patrick M'Carroll,	do.	do. ...	do. ...
	329	"	William Mills, ...	do.	do. ...	do. ...
Assistant Commissioners—						
J. H. Ross (Legal). G. A. G. Adamson. W. Jeffcott.	281	Apr. 6,	Simon Dalton, ...	M. J. Burnside, ...	Clones, ...	Drumsw[illegible],
	173	"	Margaret Cosgrove,	Henry Smith, ...	do. ...	Cranbane, ...
	165	"	Philip Martin, ...	do.	do. ...	Cavany, ...
	167	"	Samuel Armstrong,	Thos. Coote and another,	Cootehill, ...	Drumate Tyugh and another.
	1[illegible]	"	Thomas Bell, ...	Earl of Dartrey, ...	Monaghan,	Rairnes and another.
	179	"	John Dalton, ...	Henry Smith, ...	Clones, ...	Cranbane, ...
						Total, ...

COUNTY OF

Names of Assistant Commissioners by whom Cases were decided.	Record Number.	Date of Order.	Name of Tenant.	Name of Landlord.	Poor Law Union.	Townland.
Assistant Commissioners—	200	Apr. 23,	Edward Teague, ...	Capt. Wm. B. Collum, ...	Irvinestown,	Raleigh Oughment.
C. H. Thomas (Legal). H. Johnston. O. M'Elderry.	201	"	John Allen, ...	William Wilson, ...	do. ...	Cabra Lea, ...
	219	"	Jane Maxwell, ...	do.	do. ...	do. ...
	1[illegible]	"	Patrick M'Caughey, continued by Patk. M'Elroy.	Dr. Robert Trimble, ...	Clogher, ...	Ballinagurragh.
	173	"	William Hackett, ...	Colonel Irvine, ...	do. ...	Mullaghmore.
	225	"	Edward M'Carroll,	Sir John Esmonde, Bart.,	do. ...	Mullans, ...
	100	"	Robert Pauley, ...	Francis P. Gervais, ...	do. ...	Edenmore, ...
	103	"	Rev. Robt. Warnock,	do.	do. ...	do. ...
	102	"	Terence O'Hagan, ...	do.	do. ...	Carnmore, ...
	164	"	James M'Girr, ...	do.	do. ...	Glencurragh.
	434	"	Daniel M'Gurley, ...	do.	do. ...	Lisnarable, ...
	302	"	James Donnelly, ...	Anne Caithness and others,	do. ...	[illegible]
	279	"	Bernard Maguire, ...	do.	do. ...	do. ...
	303	"	Catherine Collins,	do.	do. ...	do. ...
	300	"	Michael M'Glone, ...	do.	do. ...	do. ...

SECOND STATUTORY TERM.

MONAGHAN—*continued.*

Extent of Holding (Statute).	Poor Law Valuation.	Rent of Holding prior to commencement of First Statutory Term.	Judicial Rent for First Statutory Term.	Judicial Rent for Second Statutory Term.	Decrease %. on First Statutory Term.	Observations.
A. R. P.	£ s. d.	£ s. d.	£ s. d.	£ s. d.		
11 3 36	unascertained	5 14 10	3 10 0	2 16 11	63	
4 1 2	2 0 0	2 16 9	2 0 0	1 7 7	73	
16 2 12	5 10 0	10 6 8	5 5 0	4 8 8	63	
14 2 0	5 15 0	5 8 10	5 0 0	3 9 10	61	
8 1 14	1 10 0	1 2 10	1 10 0	1 4 10	58	
17 3 30	10 15 0	13 11 2	10 0 0	7 14 1	76	
7 3 37	6 10 0	10 13 0	7 0 0	4 9 0	611	
17 1 16	13 10 0	15 16 0	11 5 6	7 18 0	625	
17 2 10	18 15 0	14 10 5	13 8 5	7 10 0	256	
117 3 23	45 18 0	117 3 8	100 0 0	80 16 0	663	
34 2 16	65 6 0	88 0 0	24 13 6	18 10 0	630	
6 2 30	4 13 0	8 8 0	7 6 6	6 12 0	627	
368 3 27	368 0 0	488 10 1	309 8 11	260 16 5		

SECOND STATUTORY TERM.

COUNTY OF

Names of Assistant Commissioners by whom Cases were decided.	Record Number	Date of Order	Name of Tenant.	Name of Landlord.	Poor Law Union.	Townland.
Assistant Commissioners—		1897.				
G. H. Tuthill (Legal). H. Jephson. G. M'Elligott.	607	Apr. 23,	Michael O'Hanna, Admr. of John O'Hanna,	Anne Cairns & others, ...	Clogher, ...	Killeenhugue
	305	"	Terence Rafferty, ...	do.	do. ...	do. ...
	325	"	William M'Caw, ...	do.	do. ...	do. ...
	718	"	John M'Caughey,	do.	do. ...	do. ...
	810	"	Joseph Donnelly, ...	do.	do. ...	do. ...
	704	"	Hugh Treanor, ...	do.	do. ...	do. ...
	299	"	Peter Donaghy, ...	do.	do. ...	do. ...
	103	"	Robert Fleming, ...	do.	do. ...	Killeenhugue
	811	"	John O. M'Caughey,	do.	do. ...	do. ...
	818	"	Thomas M'Caughey, Admr. of Thomas M'Caughey, decd.	do.	do. ...	do. ...
	304	"	Arthur Donaghy, ...	do.	do. ...	do. ...
J. R. Ross (Legal). J. Rowlin.	137	Apr. 27,	James Cowan, ...	Rev. A. S. Lewis, ...	Dungannon,	Tullyodonnell,
	139	"	John Kelly, ...	do.	do. ...	do. ...
	280	"	George Anderson,	James Bruce, ...	do. ...	Carrowreagh,
	340	"	William Cardwell,	Mrs. Katherine Ross, ...	do. ...	Lower Cav, ...
	642	"	Mary M'Grath, ...	do.	do. ...	do. ...
	853	"	Edward Donnelly,	do.	do. ...	do. ...
	238	"	Abraham Nelson, ...	do.	do. ...	Drumreel Cross,
	239	"	William J. Flood, ...	do.	do. ...	Lower Cav, ...
	782	"	Ross Cotter, ...	Lord Ranfurly, ...	do. ...	Derrygeeraghy,
	434	"	Joseph M'Clean and another,	Rev. James Hamilton,	do. ...	Clogam, ...
J. W. Ross (Legal). J. Rowlin. W. Shaw.	332	Mar. 31,	James M'Garland,	Right Hon. Viscount Charlemont,	Dungannon,	Ballyward, ...
	348	"	Patrick M'Hugh, ...	James A. King & anr.,	do. ...	Drumcolly, ...
	379	"	David Ewing, ...	do.	do. ...	do. ...
	216	"	Lawrence Quinn, ...	Colonel J. C. Lowry, ...	do. ...	Kerrib, ...
	217	"	Anne M'Crory, Ltd. Admix. of John M'Crory, decd.	do.	do. ...	do. ...
	175	"	Hugh Scott, ...	Lady Adela Goff, ...	do. ...	Mullyroddan.
	[illegible]	Apr. 27,	James Ferguson, ...	Lord Ranfurly, ...	do. ...	Lisnahurry,

SECOND STATUTORY TERM.

TYRONE—*continued.*

Extent of Holding Statute.	Poor Law Valuation.	Rent of Holding prior to creation of First Statutory Term.	Judicial Rent for First Statutory Term.	Judicial Rent for Second Statutory Term.	Record No. First Statutory Term.	Observations.
A. R. P.	£ s. d.	£ s. d.	£ s. d.	£ s. d.		
28 0 15	10 10 0	11 10 0	8 10 0	8 5 6	615	
15 0 19	8 10 0	9 16 6	7 10 0	6 11 0	613	
24 2 8	13 5 0	15 5 6	12 0 0	11 0 0	611	
16 0 25	8 0 0	11 18 9	8 10 0	7 10 0	621	
10 3 30	5 5 0	6 14 10	5 4 0	4 14 0	618	
28 1 15	18 0 0	16 5 6	10 15 0	10 5 6	616	
14 0 25	9 5 0	11 1 7	8 10 0	6 10 0	624	
22 1 15	18 0 0	16 5 8	18 0 0	10 12 6	670	
15 1 25	8 0 0	10 4 3	7 10 0	7 0 0	620	
16 3 25	8 0 0	13 9 7	9 0 0	7 10 0	622	
24 2 15	11 0 0	14 12 8	11 10 0	10 5 6	610	
7 0 18	7 5 0	6 1 0	7 0 0	5 0 0	1059	
6 2 30	7 5 10	10 15 2	5 10 0	4 17 0	1062	
38 1 25	unascertained.	52 10 0	34 0 0	29 10 0	2773	
5 3 25	6 5 0	10 10 0	7 0 0	5 5 0	2228	
1 2 0	8 10 0	7 10 0	5 13 0	4 3 0	2120	
6 0 20	7 10 0	14 14 0	10 0 0	8 10 0	2254	
17 1 20	20 15 0	20 0 0	19 0 0	15 0 0	1009	
8 1 20	7 15 0	15 4 0	10 10 0	7 0 0	2221	
17 1 16	16 10 0	17 17 0	14 8 0	13 14 0	2861	
31 1 5	20 5 0	31 14 6	27 0 0	23 9 0	2616	
11 3 25	5 15 0	6 5 0	7 0 0	5 7 6	2416	
11 1 4	7 5 0	5 16 8	6 10 0	5 18 3	670	
38 0 7	32 16 0	38 11 1	28 10 0	34 5 0	671	
15 1 20	14 10 0	17 5 5	13 4 8	10 18 6	2139	
17 1 33	12 0 0	16 0 0	13 10 0	9 9 0	2132	
45 0 0	27 0 0	28 4 0	23 13 0	19 12 0	734	
27 3 33	28 10 0	30 5 0	25 0 0	22 2 0	843	

SECOND STATUTORY TERM.

COUNTY OF

Names of Assistant Commissioners by whom Cases were decided.	Record Number.	Date of Order.	Name of Tenant.	Name of Landlord.	Poor Law Union.	Townland.
Assistant Commissioners—		1897.				
O. H. Teeling (Legal). A. E. Montgomery. R. W. Crabbe.	214	April 10	Jas. Early, ...	Alex. O. L. M'Clintock,	Omagh, ...	[illegible], ...
	111	"	John Smith, ...	Archibald Warnock, ...	do. ...	[illegible]
	225	"	Patrick Teague, ...	do.	do. ...	do. ...
	272	"	John Corrigan, ...	Rev. Canon G. Tottenham and another.	do. ...	Glengun, ...
	215	"	Wm. Corrigan, ...	do.	do. ...	do. ...
	216	"	John Corrigan, ...	do.	do. ...	do. ...
	116	"	Terence M'Guigan,	Gordon Douglas and ors., Trus. of G. W. L. O'Gilby's Estate.	do. ...	[illegible], ...
	179	"	John Cox, ...	do.	do. ...	[illegible], ...
	118	"	Fran. M'Aneh, ...	do.	do. ...	[illegible], ...
	290	"	John Donk, ...	Edward Downes Martin,	do. ...	Drumragh, ...
	280	"	Wm. Donk, ...	do.	do. ...	do. ...
	183	"	Patk. M'Veigh, Lad. Admor. of David M'Veigh, deceased.	do.	do. ...	do. ...
	120	"	Wm. Armstrong, ...	Mrs. Robinson, C. A. H. G. Haldane and ano.	do. ...	[illegible] ...
	185	"	Thos. M'Guigan, ...	John S. Dunsley, ...	do. ...	[illegible],
	186	"	Daniel M'Elroy, ...	do.	do. ...	Carbally, ...
	257	"	Mary M'Cusker, ...	do.	do. ...	do. ...
	282	"	Patrick M'Quade, ...	do.	do. ...	Knockmore,
	281	"	Fran. M'Quade, ...	do.	do. ...	do. ...
	183	"	John Campbell, ...	do.	do. ...	Carbally, ...
	184	"	Terence M'Cusker,	do.	do. ...	do. ...
	291	"	Robert Quinn, ...	Major Robt. S. Hamilton,	do. ...	Aghnamoe, ...
	240	"	Richard Loughran,	do.	do. ...	do. ...
	236	"	Wm. Cassidy, ...	do.	do. ...	do. ...
	237	"	George Brown, ...	Saml. Hamilton and others,	do. ...	Augheild, ...
	432	"	Robt. Armstrong, Lad. Admor. of David Armstrong, deceased.	Harriett H. Scott, ...	do. ...	[illegible].
	433	"	John Jas. M'Nulty,	do.	do. ...	do. ...
	431	"	David Kerr, ...	do.	do. ...	do. ...
	429	"	Mary M'Quade, ...	do.	do. ...	do. ...
	437	"	Thos. M'Caffrey, ...	do.	do. ...	do. ...
	213a	"	Jas. Hawkins, ...	Alex. O. S. M'Clintock,	do. ...	Fenny, ...
	213a	"	John Hawkins, junr.,	do.	do. ...	do. ...
	228	"	Wm. Early, ...	do.	do. ...	[illegible]. ...

SECOND STATUTORY TERM.

TYRONE—*continued.*

Extent of Holding in Statute Acres.	Poor Law Valuation.	Rent of Holding prior to operation of First Statutory Term.	Judicial Rent for First Statutory Term.	Judicial Rent for Second Statutory Term.	Record No. First Statutory Term.	Observations.
A. R. P.	£ s. d.	£ s. d.	£ s. d.	£ s. d.		
23 0 0	8 10 0	18 16 0	10 16 0	8 8 0	8087	
40 0 0	24 10 0	22 6 6	18 10 0	17 10 6	1280	
27 0 0	23 10 0	28 0 0	16 10 6	19 10 6	1804	
10 1 20	10 0 0	10 5 8	8 7 6	7 0 0	1074	
21 3 20	9 10 0	13 11 0	8 0 0	8 16 8	281	
4 0 30	6 0 6	8 14 0	4 0 0	8 10 0	347	
18 0 18	14 18 0	17 10 0	18 0 0	9 16 0	6317	
14 8 25	18 10 0	16 10 0	14 0 0	11 8 6	2802	
44 8 0	69 10 0	86 16 10	65 0 0	18 11 6	2186	
18 2 10	14 6 0	18 10 6	18 8 8	10 8 0	2188	
16 1 28	11 8 0	18 0 0	11 8 0	9 10 6	2181	
8 3 0	7 0 0	7 10 0	8 0 0	4 4 6	960	
70 0 20	88 0 0	68 0 0	67 10 0	38 1 0	8427	
46 0 6	19 18 0	30 0 0	18 10 0	14 6 0	1469	
38 3 5	13 0 0	20 0 0	16 0 0	11 0 0	1714	
18 0 29	11 16 0	24 4 0	10 10 0	6 6 6	623	
63 0 0	31 0 0	38 10 0	24 10 6	19 6 0	8871	
7 3 13	Unascertained.	6 10 0	8 0 8	3 10 0	2804	
25 0 30	16 7 0	28 8 4	18 0 0	12 9 0	618	
13 3 8	4 0 0	11 0 0	7 10 0	6 15 0	611	
14 3 33	11 15 0	14 10 0	10 18 0	7 10 0	1041	
79 1 16	98 6 0	69 17 6	63 0 0	16 10 0	1864	
13 1 16	9 18 0	11 16 6	6 0 0	6 6 0	1566	
19 0 0	11 10 0	15 0 6	18 0 0	9 6 0	459	
65 3 36	16 15 0	18 0 0	14 10 0	10 0 0	2614	
15 3 19	18 0 0	14 18 0	9 0 0	6 12 0	8963	
4 3 0	5 10 0	4 10 0	8 0 6	6 6 0	3691	
16 1 0	11 10 0	14 19 0	8 10 8	7 0 0	2810	
64 8 0	18 5 0	21 0 0	18 0 0	10 0 0	2618	
37 1 6	10 0 0	13 5 0	5 6 0	6 8 6	880	
60 0 20	19 15 0	22 0 0	16 6 8	19 9 6	869	
17 0 31	5 6 0	8 15 0	6 16 0	5 10 0	3090	

SECOND STATUTORY TERM.

COUNTY OF

Names of Assistant Commissioners by whom Cases were decided.	Record Number.	Date of Order.	Name of Tenant.	Name of Landlord.	Poor Law Union.	Townland.
Assistant Commissioners—		1897.				
G. H. Tennant (Legal). A. R. Macdonnell. S. W. Chambers.	788	April 8,	Bernard Gleakin, ...	John Love, ...	Omagh, ...	Edergole, ...
	773	"	Robert M'Cutcheon,	Henry F. Crawford, ...	do. ...	Beragh, ...
	905	"	James Shearin, ...	Henry H. Stewart, ...	do. ...	[illegible], ...
	895	"	Bernard Hughes, ...	do.	do. ...	Gortin, ...
	898	"	Patrick Rafferty, ...	do.	do. ...	[illegible], ...
	897	"	John Bradley. ...	do.	do. ...	do. ...
	896	"	Terence M'Garrity.	do.	do. ...	do. ...
	899	"	Fras. Rafferty, Ltd. Admor. of Pat. Rafferty, deceased.	do.	do. ...	do. ...
	900	"	Michael M'Garrity.	do.	do. ...	Gortfin, ...
	902	"	Michael M'Cartan,	do.	do. ...	do. ...
	903	"	Charles Rafferty, ...	do.	do. ...	do. ...
	904	"	Charles Gormley, ...	do.	do. ...	[illegible], ...
	894	"	Michael M'Cartan,	do.	do. ...	do. ...
	800	"	James Fyfe, senior,	John S. Galbraith, ...	do. ...	[illegible], ...
	438	"	James Fenton, ...	Rev. P. Hackett, c.c., ...	do. ...	[illegible], ...
	429	"	Stewart Parry, ...	Matthew Campbell, ...	do. ...	[illegible],
	414	"	John Johnston, ...	Rose and Mary Kelly, ...	do. ...	Edergole, ...
	391	"	Patrick Gallagher.	W. S. Corry, a minor, by Mrs. Charlotte Corry, his Guardian, ad litem.	do. ...	[illegible], ...
	427	"	Joseph Caldwell, ...	William Arnott Harvey,	do. ...	[illegible], ...
	460	"	Fras. Henderson & another.	Samuel Johnston, ...	do. ...	[illegible],
	387	"	Patrick M'Glone, ...	Col. William Clarke, ...	do. ...	[illegible], ...
	805	"	James Hamilton, ...	Hugh Wargrath & anor.,	do. ...	[illegible], ...
	178	"	Jas. M'Loughlin, ...	Rev. G. Irvine, ...	do. ...	[illegible], ...
	215	"	Robert Patton, ...	Dr. Thomas Scott, ...	do. ...	[illegible], ...
	105	"	George Armstrong,	James Houston & anor.,	do. ...	[illegible], ...
	344	"	Peter Rafferty and anor., Ltd. Admors. of Hugh Rafferty, deceased.	Earl of Belmore, ...	do. ...	[illegible], ...
	[illegible]	Mar. 23,	Henry O'Neill, ...	Gordon Douglas & others, Trustees of Estate of G. W. L. O'Gilby.	do. ...	[illegible], ...
	311	"	Edward Connolly,	Mrs. S. C. A. H. C. [illegible] and another.	do. ...	[illegible], ...
	[illegible]	Jan. 27,	Samuel Wilson, ...	Gordon Douglas & others, Trustees of Estate of G. W. L. O'Gilby.	do. ...	[illegible], ...
	183	Mar. 22,	James M'Clung, ...	do.	do. ...	[illegible], ...
	177	"	Nicholas Smith, ...	do.	do. ...	[illegible], ...

SECOND STATUTORY TERM.

TYRONE—*continued.*

Extent of Holding. Statute.	Poor Law Valuation.	Rent of Holding prior to commencement of First Statutory Term.	Judicial Rent for First Statutory Term.	Judicial Rent for Second Statutory Term.	Record No. First Statutory Term.	Observations.
A. R. P.	£ s. d.	£ s. d.	£ s. d.	£ s. d.		
17 0 30	18 15 0	18 0 0	11 10 0	9 10 0	2251	By consent.
30 1 30	15 0 0	12 0 0	17 10 0	14 0 0	2077	do.
15 0 10	5 0 0	7 0 0	4 0 0	3 0 0	1665	do.
5 3 5	5 0 0	4 0 0	3 15 0	3 4 0	1673	do.
13 0 30	7 0 0	0 0 0	6 0 0	5 0 0	1795	do.
12 0 10	5 0 0	7 0 0	5 0 0	4 0 0	1689	do.
18 1 30	8 0 0	10 3 5	5 0 0	5 0 0	1691	do.
17 0 35	8 5 0	10 0 0	7 5 0	5 10 0	1680	do.
18 0 25	9 10 0	10 0 0	7 10 0	5 4 0	1681	do.
13 1 15	5 5 0	5 5 0	4 15 0	3 12 0	1685	do.
16 1 0	8 5 0	11 7 0	8 0 0	5 0 0	1690	do
26 3 30	17 15 0	22 10 0	15 0 0	12 15 0	1593	do.
20 1 6	14 0 0	14 0 0	11 10 0	8 4 0	1694	do
35 3 39	29 2 0	26 18 11	23 10 0	16 0 0	1615	do.
80 0 30	40 0 0	47 5 0	41 0 0	38 0 0	225	
86 0 0	80 0 0	45 0 0	34 0 0	25 16 8	785	
64 1 15	unascertained.	12 0 0	83 0 0	22 2 0	773	
10 2 20	6 0 0	4 10 0	5 0 0	4 8 0	2263	
79 1 23	84 0 0	65 3 4	51 0 0	41 5 6	143	
35 3 10	91 0 0	80 10 0	91 10 0	14 0 0	2085	
9 0 18	6 8 0	8 0 0	7 0 0	6 0 9	18	
80 1 20	19 16 0	23 6 0	16 0 0	13 6 0	2084	
24 0 35	17 0 0	18 10 0	15 0 0	13 0 0	7797	
35 3 20	13 10 0	20 0 0	14 0 0	10 15 5	2389	
19 0 25	11 0 0	17 0 0	13 10 0	8 15 5	315	
16 0 10	9 15 0	10 10 0	8 0 8	6 14 0	1648	
7 0 35	3 0 0	5 5 5	4 0 0	3 10 0	5180	
34 2 20	18 0 0	15 0 0	13 0 0	10 4 0	2093	
80 0 10	31 5 0	39 14 1	81 0 0	24 10 0	3173	By consent.
25 2 20	18 5 0	24 11 4	18 10 0	14 0 0	2298	
80 0 25	14 9 0	47 1 1	32 10 0	24 0 0	2201	

SECOND STATUTORY TERM.

COUNTY OF

Names of Assistant Commissioners by whom Cases were decided.	Record Number.	Date of Order.	Name of Tenant.	Name of Landlord.	Poor Law Union.	Townland.
Assistant Commissioners—		1887.				
C. H. Teeling (Legal). A. S. Montgomery. E. W. Crawford.	116	Mar. 22,	Robert T. Kerr, ...	Gordon Douglas and ors., Trustees of Estate of C. W. L. O'Gilby.	Omagh, ...	Rahony, ...
	207	,,	James Wilson, ...	do.	do. ...	Garvagh, ...
	189	,,	John Orr, ...	do.	do. ...	Lisnamuck, ...
	179	,,	James Teague, ...	do.	do. ...	Rahony, ...
	175	,,	John Smith, ...	do.	do. ...	do. ...
	59	,,	Patrick M'Aleer, ...	Alexander C. S. M'Causland.	do. ...	Drumnakilly.
	120	,,	Peter Daly & ors.,	do.	do. ...	do. ...
	181	,,	Hugh Daly, ...	do.	do. ...	do. ...
	160	,,	James Kelly, ...	do.	do. ...	Cloughfin, ...
	231	,,	John Kerr, ...	do.	do. ...	Killycurragh, ...
	278	,,	John Daly (Savamore),	do.	do. ...	Drumnakilly.
	426	,,	Patrick M'Aleer, ...	do.	do. ...	do. ...
	165	,,	David Kyle, ...	Elizabeth J. M'Causland,	do. ...	do. ...
	423	,,	Francis M'Veigh, ...	Rose M'Mackin, a minor, by Mrs. A. M'Mackin, her Mother & Guardian.	do. ...	Edergold, ...
	302	,,	Patrick Mellon, ...	do.	do. ...	Corrales, ...
	115	,,	James Gillespie, ...	Earl of Belmore, ...	do. ...	Ballintrain, ...
	219	,,	Arthur Owens, ...	do.	do. ...	Rograndum, ...
	411	,,	Andrew Irvine, ...	Emily Walworth & ors.,	do. ...	Aughagallon.
	412	,,	James I. Ramsey, ...	do.	do. ...	do. ...
	317	,,	Robert M'Ghee, ...	do.	do. ...	Gallally, ...
	414	Feb. 23,	David Graham, ...	do.	do. ...	Aughagallon.
C. H. Teeling (Legal). A. B. Montgomery. W. S. Hunt.	137	Apr. 10,	James Rutledge, ...	Alexander C. S. M'Causland.	Omagh, ...	Fauny, ...
	618	,,	Francis M'Cartney,	Mrs. Elizabeth Ellen M'Cartney.	do. ...	Lisnacreaght, ...
C. H. Teeling (Legal). W. S. Hunt.	104	Apr. 9,	John Baxter, ...	Ashley S. T. J. Leary & another.	Castlederg.	Magheracreggan, ...
C. H. Teeling (Legal). G. N. Caldwell. W. S. Hunt.	417	Mar. 30,	John Pigott, ...	Gordon Douglas and ors., Trustees of Estate of C. W. L. O'Gilby.	Omagh, ...	Meenyoarrow.
	346	,,	Phillip Meehan, ...	George Agnew, ...	Castlederg, ...	Edenreagh, ...
	345	,,	Michael M'Philomy,	do.	do. ...	do. ...

SECOND STATUTORY TERM.

TYRONE—continued.

Extent of Holding. Statute.	Poor Law Valuation.	Rent of Holding prior to creation of First Statutory Term.	Judicial Rent for First Statutory Term.	Judicial Rent for Second Statutory Term.	Record No. First Statutory Term.	Observations.
A. R. P.	£ s. d.	£ s. d.	£ s. d.	£ s. d.		
[illegible] 3 16	63 10 0	45 0 0	[illegible] 0 0	[illegible] 9 0	3190	
67 [illegible] 0	33 0 0	40 [illegible] 0	[illegible] 0 0	[illegible] 17 0	[illegible]	
18 1 0	[illegible] 10 0	10 3 0	6 0 0	[illegible] 15 0	[illegible]	
[illegible] 0 0	12 15 0	[illegible] 10 5	17 10 0	12 0 0	2315	
[illegible] 0 0	21 10 0	[illegible] 0 0	27 10 0	18 10 0	2316	
[illegible] 0 17	10 5 0	14 0 0	5 10 0	5 15 0	[illegible]	
34 0 18	unascertained,	18 18 0	17 0 0	10 10 0	4148	
18 0 0	6 0 0	6 1 0	5 10 9	4 0 6	4154	
[illegible] 1 [illegible]	5 10 0	15 15 0	[illegible] 10 0	5 0 0	[illegible]	
40 1 [illegible]	8 10 0	13 4 0	8 10 0	5 15 0	4178	
17 0 0	6 0 0	5 0 0	[illegible] 0 0	4 15 9	[illegible]	
48 1 3	18 10 0	21 5 0	16 0 0	18 0 0	4181	
[illegible] 2 10	5 10 0	11 7 0	8 5 0	9 15 0	2643	
[illegible] [illegible] [illegible]	16 0 0	37 0 0	15 10 0	19 0 0	473	
[illegible] [illegible] 30	61 15 0	[illegible] 0 0	25 0 0	20 0 0	673	
47 1 [illegible]	17 15 0	25 13 0	23 0 0	17 3 0	4270	
[illegible] 0 0	18 0 0	19 0 0	11 0 0	5 14 5	3545	
13 1 [illegible]	unascertained,	13 1 0	16 10 0	[illegible]	607	By consent.
43 0 0	do.	41 17 0	31 10 0	[illegible] 4 0	616	do.
30 [illegible] [illegible]	do.	29 15 3	22 10 0	18 0 0	610	do.
31 4 0	30 0 0	[illegible] 10 0	24 10 0	19 13 0	415	do.
30 0 [illegible]	15 5 0	[illegible] 0 0	15 0 0	10 0 0	[illegible]	
15 0 0	7 5 0	14 5 0	5 10 0	4 0 0	580	
61 0 0	14 15 0	18 7 0	17 0 0	7 0 0	[illegible]	

SECOND STATUTORY TERM.

COUNTY OF

Names of Assistant Commissioners by whom Cases were heard.	Record Number.	Date of Order.	Name of Tenant.	Name of Landlord.	Poor Law Union.	Townland.
Assistant Commissioners—		1877.				
C. H. Tyrrell (Legal). G. N. Caldwell. W. S. Hunt.	263	Mar. 30,	William J. Semple,	George Agnew, ...	Castlederg,	Edenmagh, ...
	243	„	Margaret Maguire,	do.	do. ...	do. ...
	264	„	John M'Crory, ...	do.	do. ...	do. ...
	241	„	James M'Menamin,	do.	do. ...	do. ...
	181	„	Andrew Sandgrove,	John Colquhoun, ...	Strabane, ...	Ballymaleen ...
C. H. Tyrrell (Legal). A. E. Montgomery. R. W. Chamney	105	Mar. 22,	John M'Menamin,	Mrs. Frith Thompson, ...	Omagh, ...	Pollnet, ...
	107	„	James Slevin, ...	do.	do. ...	do. ...
	109	„	Francis M'Caley,	do.	do. ...	do. ...
	108	„	Patrick Maldeen, ...	do.	do. ...	do. ...
	107	„	Patrick O'Reilly, ...	do.	do. ...	do. ...
	110	„	Francis Donaghy,	do.	do. ...	do. ...
	111	„	Mary M'Menamin,	Mrs. Margaret Thompson,	do. ...	do. ...
						Total, ...

PROVINCE OF

COUNTY OF

Names of Assistant Commissioners by whom Cases were heard.	Record Number.	Date of Order.	Name of Tenant.	Name of Landlord.	Poor Law Union.	Townland.
Assistant Commissioners—	1	Apr. 20,	John Farrell, ...	Maria S. Butler, ...	Balrothery,	Walshtown, ...
L. Doyle (Legal). A. N. Curtis. G. S. Bolster.	5	„	Bartholw. Murray, ...	Annie S. M. Baker and ano., Minors, by Annie Caterson, their Guardian.	do. ...	Gaprolagh, ...
	6	„	Joseph Moore, ...	do.	do. ...	do. ...
	8	„	Mary Wallace, ...	do.	do. ...	do. ...
						Total, ...

KINGS

Names of Assistant Commissioners by whom Cases were heard.	Record Number.	Date of Order.	Name of Tenant.	Name of Landlord.	Poor Law Union.	Townland.
Assistant Commissioners—	10	April 9,	Timothy Carey, ...	Henry S. Palmer, ...	Roscrea, ...	Ballymurphy & another.
M. T. Craig (Legal). F. M. Carroll. J. Hawkins.	9	„	Patrick Cussane, ...	Earl of Rosse, ...	do. ...	Meyanna, ...
						Total, ...

SECOND STATUTORY TERM.

TYRONE—*continued.*

Extent of Holding. Statute Measure.	Poor Law Valuation.	Rent of Holding prior to commencement of First Statutory Term.	Judicial Rent for First Statutory Term.	Judicial Rent for Second Statutory Term.	Record No. [illegible] Statutory Term.	Observations.
A. R. P.	£ s. d.	£ s. d.	£ s. d.	£ s. d.		
21 0 10	16 5 0	23 10 0	15 0 0	11 0 0	257	
18 2 20	9 10 6	13 10 0	9 10 6	7 5 0	239	
34 0 0	18 0 0	21 0 0	17 0 0	13 0 0	840	
7 3 16	5 0 0	6 15 8	4 15 0	3 10 0	836	
14 3 30	23 3 0	47 17 6	35 0 0	27 5 0	2894	
8 0 0	5 15 0	6 10 4	6 15 0	4 5 0	1915	
68 2 20	26 5 0	27 18 0	23 15 0	16 0 0	1918	
11 1 4	7 5 0	7 5 0	6 12 6	4 12 0	1919	
81 1 25	16 10 0	18 5 8	15 5 0	10 0 0	1916	
30 0 30	18 0 0	13 11 5	11 9 5	8 5 0	1920	
17 1 28	11 15 0	13 14 10	10 10 0	7 14 0	1921	
16 3 26	11 5 0	11 6 9	8 0 0	6 0 0	1917	
3,[illegible] 0 36	2,078 18 10	2,773 3 9½	2,114 7 3	1,681 6 4		

LEINSTER.

DUBLIN.

Extent of Holding. Statute Measure.	Poor Law Valuation.	Rent of Holding prior to commencement of First Statutory Term.	Judicial Rent for First Statutory Term.	Judicial Rent for Second Statutory Term.	Record No. [illegible] Statutory Term.	Observations.
29 1 7	23 0 0	34 0 0	31 10 0	27 5 0	84	
13 3 8	10 5 0	18 15 0	17 15 0	13 0 0	65	
10 1 0	13 0 0	22 0 0	23 0 0	16 10 0	97	
67 3 13	41 0 0	88 5 0	80 0 0	48 0 0	85	
109 0 21	87 5 0	164 0 0	151 5 0	98 15 0		

COUNTY.

SECOND STATUTORY TERM.

COUNTY OF

Names of Assistant Commissioners by whom Cases were decided.	Record Number.	Date of Order.	Name of Tenant.	Name of Landlord.	Poor Law Union.	Townland.
		1887.				
Assistant Commissioners—	3	April 9,	Michael Dillon, ...	William H. Fairclough,	[illegible], ...	[illegible],
E. T. Crean (Legal). James D. Boyd. J. [illegible].	8	"	Margaret Connolly, Ltd. Admix. of Owen M'Guffin,	do.	do. ...	do. ...
	1	"	James Sheridan, ...	Nicholas Halligan, ...	do. ...	[illegible], ...
	19	"	Catherine M'Ateer,	Maria Wilson & others, Trustees of Mrs. Elizabeth M'Clenaghan.	[illegible], ...	[illegible], ...
	18	"	Daniel Christy, ...	do.	do. ...	do. ...
	16	"	James Thompson,	do.	do. ...	do. ...
	10	"	Lawrence Berry, ...	do.	do. ...	do. ...
	14	"	Patrick Loughran,	do.	do. ...	do. ...
	15	"	Catherine Kinn, ...	do.	do. ...	do. ...
	13	"	Bridget M'Kevitt,	do.	do. ...	do. ...
	11	"	Patrick Duggan, Ltd. Admix. of [illegible] Daly.	do.	do. ...	do. ...
	10	"	Mary Kenny, ...	do.	do. ...	do. ...
	9	"	Patrick Loughran,	do.	do. ...	do. ...
	8	"	Patrick King, ...	do.	do. ...	do. ...
	7	"	James M'Kevitt, ...	do.	do. ...	do. ...
	6	"	James M'Enery, ...	do.	do. ...	do. ...
	6	"	Laurence Loughran,	do.	do. ...	do. ...
	4	"	Thomas M'Nally,	do.	do. ...	do. ...
						Total, ...

COUNTY OF

Names of Assistant Commissioners by whom Cases were decided.	Record Number.	Date of Order.	Name of Tenant.	Name of Landlord.	Poor Law Union.	Townland.
Assistant Commissioners—	1	April 9,	Patrick M'Cullen,	Ralph Smith, ...	Drogheda,	[illegible], ...
E. T. Crean (Legal). J. D. Boyd. J. [illegible].	3	"	John Walsh, ...	Mrs. Caroline D. [illegible],	Ardee, ...	[illegible],
	2	"	Mrs. [illegible], Ltd. Admix. of Mrs. Mary Russell,	do.	do. ...	do. ...
	4	"	John Curry, ...	James T. [illegible], ...	do. ...	[illegible],
						Total, ...

SECOND STATUTORY TERM.

LOUTH.

Extent of Holding. Statute.	Poor Law Valuation.	Rent of Holding prior to creation of First Statutory Term.	Judicial Rent for First Statutory Term.	Judicial Rent for Second Statutory Term.	Record No. First Statutory Term.	Observations.
A. R. P.	£ s. d.	£ s. d.	£ s. d.	£ s. d.		
6 3 17	4 0 0	6 6 6	5 0 0	4 0 0	181	
8 0 31	6 0 0	8 2 8	6 0 0	4 10 0	180	
30 1 28	26 10 0	34 6 0	30 0 0	34 0 0	82	
7 0 0	4 5 0	6 0 0	4 0 0	3 10 0	178	
11 3 15	6 5 0	11 7 6	7 6 0	6 10 0	177	
6 7 25	3 15 0	7 5 0	4 10 0	3 15 0	175	
13 0 0	3 0 0	5 0 0	6 0 0	2 15 0	173	
7 2 0	8 5 0	5 6 0	5 6 0	3 11 4	171	
8 1 0	4 10 0	6 4 8	4 0 0	3 15 0	170	
4 3 34	3 5 0	5 18 0	3 3 0	2 18 0	136	
4 1 0	2 10 0	8 6 0	2 5 0	2 0 0	184	
6 3 0	5 18 0	4 16 0	6 0 0	2 10 0	84	
11 2 0	6 6 0	8 1 0	6 10 0	5 4 0	83	
7 3 19	3 5 0	6 10 0	4 0 0	3 5 0	82	
9 3 8	5 5 0	8 8 0	5 2 0	4 18 8	80	
15 0 7	7 15 0	12 16 0	8 10 0	7 4 0	79	
10 0 10	6 0 0	10 5 0	8 0 0	8 6 0	78	
2 2 24	1 15 0	2 12 8	2 0 0	1 18 8	77	
157 1 34	96 8 0	157 11 6	107 10 0	88 13 8		

MEATH.

Extent of Holding. Statute.	Poor Law Valuation.	Rent of Holding prior to creation of First Statutory Term.	Judicial Rent for First Statutory Term.	Judicial Rent for Second Statutory Term.	Record No. First Statutory Term.	Observations.
5 1 2	7 10 0	14 8 8	12 15 0	8 0 0	8	
30 0 16	26 0 0	34 10 4	84 10 4	34 10 0	184	
184 0 12	181 5 0	231 0 0	139 0 0	187 0 0	185	
40 2 1	36 0 0	77 19 0	60 10 0	61 0 0	186	
270 1 33	258 15 0	357 18 0	345 15 4	280 10 0		

COUNTY.

QUEEN'S

Names of Assistant Commissioners by whom Cases were decided.	Record Number.	Date of Order.	Name of Tenant.	Name of Landlord.	Poor Law Union.	Townland.
Assistant Commissioners—		1897.				
M. T. Crean (Legal). F. M. Gaskell. J. Hawkins.	46	April 8,	Peter Maher, ...	Robert H. Stubber, ...	Roscrea,	Clonmore and Ballinakill
	44	"	Robert Aikens, ...	do.	do. ...	Clonmore and Rossmore,
	34	"	Peter Conner, ...	do.	do. ...	Curryhill, ...
	58	"	Margaret Delaney,	Lord Digby, ...	Mountmellick,	Manison, ...
	45	"	Ephraim S. Mitchell,	Miss Emma Cornwall and another.	Roscrea, ...	Bradbury, ...
	20	"	William Phelan, ...	Eyre Coote, ...	Mountmellick,	Dysartbeagh,
	19	"	Charles Delaney, ...	Mrs. Cornelia Adair, ...	do. ...	Nyre, ...
	53	"	Bridget Dwyer, ...	Earl of Portarlington, ...	Abbeyleix,	Ironmills, ...
	8	"	Michael Brennan, ...	Miss Nannie Edge, ...	do. ...	Moyadd, ...
	7	"	Hester Byrne, ...	do.	do. ...	do. ...
	6	"	Mrs. Mary Maher,	Mrs. Emily S. Doyne, ...	do. ...	Clashavrane and Ballytag
	11	"	Mary Dowling, ...	Lord Castletown, ...	do. ...	Old Barris, ...
	12	"	James Dowling, ...	do. ...	do. ...	Cash,
	10	"	Do., ...	do. ...	do. ...	do. ...
						Total, ...

COUNTY OF

Names of Assistant Commissioners by whom Cases were decided.	Record Number.	Date of Order.	Name of Tenant.	Name of Landlord.	Poor Law Union.	Townland.
Assistant Commissioners— M. T. Crean (Legal). E. A. Dillon. J. A. O'Kelly.	14	Apr. 22,	Thomas Cook, ...	Mrs. Lucy Owen, ...	Gorey, ...	Ballytegan, ...
	19	"	Edward Doyle, ...	Earl of Courtown, ...	do. ...	Ballingale, ...
	15	"	James Connors, Leg. Admor. of Daniel Connors, deceased.	Arthur H. James, ...	Enniscorthy,	Ballycrystal,
	13	"	Patrick Kavanagh,	Walter M. Kavanagh, ...	New Ross, ...	Ballymoney.
						Total, ...

PROVINCE OF

COUNTY OF

Names of Assistant Commissioners by whom Cases were decided.	Record Number.	Date of Order.	Name of Tenant.	Name of Landlord.	Poor Law Union.	Townland.
Assistant Commissioners— L. Doyle (Legal). D. O'Keeffe. J. Reid.	82	April 2,	John M'Mahon, ...	Stephen E. Woulfe, ...	Ennis, ...	Ballyvaskin, ...
	81	"	John O'Loughlen,	Thomas C. S. Mahon, ...	Ennistymon,	Ballyna & c.
	77	"	John Kierce, ...	John F. Callinan, ...	Corofin, ...	Kilbeen,
	78	"	Cornelius Callinan,	do.	do. ...	do. ...

SECOND STATUTORY TERM.

COUNTY—*continued.*

Extent of Holding, Statute.	Poor Law Valuation.	Rent of Holding prior to creation of First Statutory Term.	Judicial Rent for First Statutory Term.	Judicial Rent for Second Statutory Term.	Record No. First Statutory Term.	Observations.
A. R. P.	£ s. d.	£ s. d.	£ s. d.	£ s. d.		
31 0 19	18 10 0	19 0 0	15 10 0	13 0 0	209	
16 0 0	33 10 0	35 7 0	35 7 0	[illegible] 0 0	916	
36 0 0	17 0 0	31 6 0	20 0 0	16 10 0	47	
167 3 26	104 10 0	183 0 4	125 0 0	118 1 6	288	
74 2 1	60 0 0	70 0 0	48 0 0	41 5 0	196	
59 1 31	31 15 0	40 15 0	29 15 0	17 17 8	167	
40 0 4	18 5 0	23 11 1	19 10 0	15 8 0	277	
11 0 14	7 10 0	10 10 0	7 10 0	7 10 0	836	
163 3 0	83 15 0	250 0 0	170 0 0	127 0 0	121	
80 3 0	64 15 0	180 0 0	100 0 0	79 0 0	183	
190 3 30	77 5 0	118 6 0	81 0 0	65 15 0	390	
18 1 0	10 0 0	8 0 0	6 10 0	6 11 0	18	
46 1 19	29 0 0	64 5 5	64 0 0	39 16 6	18	
18 0 31	10 0 0	10 0 0	8 0 0	6 0 0	10	
1,079 0 4	664 5 0	1,243 8 1	690 5 0	749 13 8		

WEXFORD.

Extent of Holding, Statute.	Poor Law Valuation.	Rent of Holding prior to creation of First Statutory Term.	Judicial Rent for First Statutory Term.	Judicial Rent for Second Statutory Term.	Record No. First Statutory Term.	Observations.
63 3 25	66 10 0	97 0 0	63 10 0	53 10 0	121	
65 3 15	47 0 0	38 18 0	60 0 0	35 10 0	146	
141 1 36	26 10 0	40 11 4	34 10 0	25 0 0	105	With right of grazing 1/11th of Ballyveryeal Mountain, containing 770a. 0r. 13p.
113 3 24	96 15 0	160 4 0	118 0 0	80 0 0	111	
382 1 14	238 15 0	353 10 4	285 0 0	195 0 0		

MUNSTER.

COUNTY OF

Names of Assistant Commissioners by whom Cases were decided.	Record Number	Date of Order.	Name of Tenant.	Name of Landlord	Poor Law Union.	Townland
Assistant Commissioners—		1897.				
L. Doyle (Legal). C. O'Keeffe. J. Rice.	107	April 2,	Patrick Carney, ...	Mary Kenny and another, reps. of Matthew Kenny,	Ennistymon,	Formoyle and ...
	29	„	John Gordon, ...	Alfred O'Brien, ...	do. ...	Moughna, ...
	35	„	Patrick Lynch, ...	do.	do. ...	do. ...
	63	„	John M'Guire, ...	do.	do. ...	do. ...
	36	„	Honoria Kennedy, Ltd. Admix. of Thomas Kennedy.	do.	do. ...	do. ...
	39	„	John Brennan, Ltd. Admix. of Michael Brennan.	do.	do. ...	do. ...
	40	„	John Vaughan, ...	do.	do. ...	do. ...
	48	„	Michael Doherty, ...	do.	do. ...	do. ...
	60	„	Terence M'Guire, ...	do.	do. ...	do. ...
	27	„	William Devereux,	do.	do. ...	Knockaskibbolyhan.
	55	„	Denis Clare, ...	Henry V. Macnamara,	do. ...	Ballyvaskane, ...
						Total, ...

COUNTY OF

Names of Assistant Commissioners by whom Cases were decided.	Record Number	Date of Order.	Name of Tenant.	Name of Landlord	Poor Law Union.	Townland
Assistant Commissioners—	130	April 9,	Daniel Shaughnessy, ...	Mary R. Whitcombe and another.	Midleton, ...	Glenbrohagh,
L. Doyle (Legal). E. G. Perry.	127	„	Patrick Moriarty, ...	Viscount Midleton, ...	do. ...	Coppingerstown.
	191	„	Thomas Brien, ...	do.	do. ...	Carrigshane,
	161	„	William Moore, ...	do.	do. ...	Knockgriffin,
	174	„	John M'Carthy, ...	do.	do. ...	Castleredmond,
	175	„	Patrick M'Carthy,	do.	do. ...	do. ...
	125	„	Ellen Kelleher, ...	do.	do. ...	Coppingerstown.
	123	„	Patrick Ahern, ...	do.	do. ...	do. ...
	178	„	Michael Hennessy, ...	William E. Bolton, ...	do. ...	Ballyspillane, ...
	177	„	Cornelius Hurley, ...	do.	do. ...	do. ...
	209	„	Michael Cahill, ...	do.	do. ...	do. ...
	183	„	John Ahern, Ltd. Admor. of Maurice Ahern.	do.	do. ...	do. ...
	181	„	James Carey, ...	do. ...	do. ...	do. ...
	180	„	Michael Carey, Ltd. Admor. of Patrick Carey.	do. ...	do. ...	do. ...
	179	„	John Quirk, ...	do.	do. ...	do. ...
						Total, ...

CLARE—*continued.*

Extent of Holding. Statute.	Poor Law Valuation.	Rent of Holding prior to fixing of First Statutory Term.	Judicial Rent for First Statutory Term.	Judicial Rent for Second Statutory Term.	Record No. First Statutory Term.	Observations.
a. r. p.	£ s. d.	£ s. d.	£ s. d.	£ s. d.		
42 0 20	9 10 0	25 0 0	15 0 0	12 0 0	[illegible]	
31 1 20	11 10 0	21 14 0	21 18 0	8 5 0	[illegible]	
22 3 20	8 10 0	17 0 0	10 10 0	8 0 0	518	With turbary for use on holding.
17 2 20	4 10 0	10 15 10	6 0 0	5 0 0	430	do.
61 2 18	15 0 0	31 17 8	20 0 0	15 0 0	483	do.
30 3 9	18 10 0	25 10 0	14 10 0	18 0 0	431	do.
63 3 6	11 10 0	23 7 3	16 0 0	9 5 0	438	
20 1 27	8 15 0	23 1 1	11 0 0	8 0 0	458	do.
21 0 17	5 15 0	14 8 0	5 0 0	6 0 0	518	do.
48 0 8	6 10 0	16 3 1	6 0 0	5 10 0	483	
16 2 15	9 18 0	13 11 0	10 10 0	8 10 0	504	
[illegible] 0 5	104 17 0	409 7 6	158 12 0	109 0 0		

CORK.

Extent of Holding. Statute.	Poor Law Valuation.	Rent of Holding prior to fixing of First Statutory Term.	Judicial Rent for First Statutory Term.	Judicial Rent for Second Statutory Term.	Record No. First Statutory Term.	Observations.
113 2 5	74 0 0	104 4 0	95 0 0	77 17 8	[illegible]	
41 2 20	64 15 0	114 18 0	93 0 0	70 0 0	[illegible]	
32 0 20	29 15 0	39 10 0	37 0 0	30 0 0	2764	
78 1 7	67 0 0	94 18 10	90 0 0	71 16 0	[illegible]	
85 1 14	60 5 0	75 0 0	65 0 0	49 10 0	[illegible]	
71 3 20	70 5 0	90 15 4	77 0 0	61 10 0	[illegible]	
84 0 18	63 10 0	115 10 4	100 0 0	80 10 0	697	
85 3 12	31 0 0	44 17 0	38 0 0	30 7 5	[illegible]	
120 0 0	84 0 0	144 0 0	102 0 0	79 10 0	[illegible]	
7 0 8	3 0 0	5 4 0	8 10 0	3 3 0	694	
85 0 0	19 0 0	23 0 0	20 0 0	14 2 6	165	
30 0 0	19 0 0	23 10 0	14 10 0	11 7 6	699	
30 0 0	10 5 0	30 0 0	18 10 0	11 0 0	698	
85 0 0	15 15 0	28 10 0	18 0 0	15 0 0	497	
31 3 0	11 18 0	17 11 0	12 10 0	11 5 0	594	
[illegible] 2 20	634 5 0	978 15 6	784 0 0	615 5 0		

CIVIL BILL

PROVINCE OF

SECOND STATUTORY TERM.

COUNTY OF

County Court Judge.	Record Number.	Date of Order.	Name of Tenant.	Name of Landlord.	Poor Law Union.	Townland.
		1877.				
D. Fitzgerald, Q.C.	48	Jan. 14,	James Phelan, ...	Miss Jane Thomas, ...	Castlecomer,	Tullowbrin, ...
	49	,,	Patrick Byrne, ...	do. ...	Kilkenny, ...	do. ...
	50	,,	Judith Byrne, ...	do. ...	do. ...	do. ...
	51	,,	William Manning,	Mrs. Eliza Bagay, ...	do. ...	Mount Nugent,
	52	,,	John Bailey, ...	do. ...	do. ...	do. ...
	53	,,	John M'Donnell, ...	do. ...	do. ...	do. ...
	54	Apr. 17,	Mary Phelan, ...	George Holy, ...	Urlingford,	Rathpelim, ...
						Total, ...

COUNTY OF

County Court Judge.	Record Number.	Date of Order.	Name of Tenant.	Name of Landlord.	Poor Law Union.	Townland.
W. H. Kenny, Q.C.	7	Apr. 24,	James Boxterly, ...	Mrs. Mackley, ...	Ardee, ...	Mooremount,
	11	,,	James Moley, ...	Major Fortescue, ...	Dundalk, ...	Killencool, ...
	12	,,	Patrick Hardy, ...	do. ...	do. ...	do. ...
	13	,,	Patrick Byrne, ...	Laurence Byrne, ...	Ardee, ...	Maine, ...
						Total, ...

PROVINCE OF

COUNTY OF

COURTS.

LEINSTER.

SECOND STATUTORY TERM.

KILKENNY.

Extent of Holding. Statute.	Poor Law Valuation.	Rent of Holding prior to creation of First Statutory Term.	Judicial Rent for First Statutory Term.	Judicial Rent for Second Statutory Term.	Record No. First Statutory Term.	Observations.
A. R. P.	£ s. d.	£ s. d.	£ s. d.	£ s. d.		
[illegible] 3 19	10 15 0	14 17 0	12 10 0	9 0 0	541 L.C.C.	
[illegible] 2 [illegible]	15 0 0	21 19 0	18 10 0	14 0 0	208 L.C.C.	
87 1 34	29 10 0	67 3 3	39 0 0	29 0 0	134 L.C.C.	
32 1 [illegible]	17 0 0	24 0 0	18 3 6	15 0 0	107 L.C.C.	
104 3 [illegible]	13 10 0	58 19 0	60 0 0	40 0 0	108 L.C.C.	
16 1 33	7 10 0	8 0 0	6 10 0	6 0 0	110 L.C.C.	
7 3 [illegible]	6 5 0	7 10 0	5 10 0	1 10 0	200 L.C.C.	
310 1 15	129 10 0	208 1 3	150 3 6	118 10 0		

LOUTH.

Extent of Holding. Statute.	Poor Law Valuation.	Rent of Holding prior to creation of First Statutory Term.	Judicial Rent for First Statutory Term.	Judicial Rent for Second Statutory Term.	Record No. First Statutory Term.	Observations.
61 1 23	56 0 0	85 10 0	72 10 0	67 8 7	121 Agt. L.C.	
51 3 26	70 0 0	108 0 6	75 0 0	60 11 3	337 Agt. L.C.	
39 3 7	40 0 0	65 3 0	47 10 0	34 0 0	200 Agt. L.C.	
13 0 11	22 5 0	32 17 0	30 0 0	28 10 3	65 L.C.C.	
176 0 [illegible]	188 5 0	291 9 8	224 0 0	178 13 1		

MUNSTER.

CORK.

SECOND STATUTORY TERM.

COUNTY OF

County Court Judge.	Record Number.	Date of Order.	Name of Tenant.	Name of Landlord.	Poor Law Union.	Townland.
		1897.				
W. S. [illegible], Q.C.	103	Jan. 23,	James Grant, ...	John St. L. Gillman, ...	Dunmanway,	Letterparran,
	60	Feb. 1,	Patrick J. Mangan,	George Fuller, ...	Skibbereen,	Derreenaliagga,
	61	Jan. 14,	John Casey, ...	Lord Ardilaun & anor.,	Macroom, ...	Clonavrie, ...
	104	Feb. 1,	John Kingston, ...	Rev. J. J. Sheehy, ...	Skibbereen,	Derryany, ...
	105	"	Timothy Leary, ...	W. T. Hungerford, ...	Schull, ...	Ballyrisode ...
						Total, ...

COUNTY OF

County Court Judge.	Record Number.	Date of Order.	Name of Tenant.	Name of Landlord.	Poor Law Union.	Townland.
J. J. Shaw, Q.C.	65	Feb. 6,	Gerald Stafford, ...	F. E. Bateman, ...	Tralee, ...	Ballinorig, ...

COUNTY OF

County Court Judge.	Record Number.	Date of Order.	Name of Tenant.	Name of Landlord.	Poor Law Union.	Townland.
R. Adams, Q.C.	123	Jan. 29,	Ellen Cusseen, ...	Capt. St. George Henry,	Limerick, ...	Singland, ...
	116	"	Do., ...	do.	do. ...	do. ...
	119	"	Michael Cusseen, ...	do.	do. ...	do. ...
	117	"	John Cusack, ...	do.	do. ...	do. ...
	137	"	James McNiece, ...	do.	do. ...	do. ...
	122	"	Daniel Reddin, ...	do.	do. ...	do. ...
	120	"	Edward Harnett, ...	do.	do. ...	do. ...
	61	Jan. 7,	Michael Hannan, ...	Robert Henry, ...	do. ...	do. ...
	60	"	James Hannan, ...	do.	do. ...	do. ...
	18	"	Mary Casey, ...	Lissamore Estate, ...	do. ...	Ballyshonin E.,
	17	"	Patrick Herbert, ...	do.	do. ...	do. ...
						Total, ...

COUNTY OF

CORK—continued.

Extent of Holding. Statute.			Poor Law Valuation.			Rent of Holding prior to execution of First Statutory Term.			Judicial Rent for First Statutory Term.			Judicial Rent for Second Statutory Term.			Record No. First Statutory Term.	Observations.
a.	r.	p.	£	s.	d.	£	s.	d.	£	s.	d.	£	s.	d.		
51	2	18	15	0	0	27	0	0	21	0	0	18	15	0	49 Agt.	
15	0	2	7	10	0	15	0	4	11	0	0	7	10	0	148 L.C.O.	
[illegible]	0	11	[illegible]	5	0	32	6	6	[illegible]	0	0	19	5	0	457 L.C.O.	
[illegible]	1	1	37	0	0	80	0	0	[illegible]	0	0	55	0	0	[illegible] L.C.O.	
15	2	0	10	0	0	68	0	0	[illegible]	0	0	21	0	0	777 L.C.O.	
[illegible]	0	35	195	5	0	331	8	8	272	0	0	187	10	0		

KERRY.

Extent of Holding. Statute.			Poor Law Valuation.			Rent of Holding prior to execution of First Statutory Term.			Judicial Rent for First Statutory Term.			Judicial Rent for Second Statutory Term.			Record No. First Statutory Term.	Observations.
51	0	[illegible]	[illegible]	15	0	37	10	4	32	0	0	60	0	0	979 L.C.O.	

LIMERICK.

Extent of Holding. Statute.			Poor Law Valuation.			Rent of Holding prior to execution of First Statutory Term.			Judicial Rent for First Statutory Term.			Judicial Rent for Second Statutory Term.			Record No. First Statutory Term.	Observations.
17	1	14	[illegible]	[illegible]	0	45	4	4	[illegible]	0	0	28	0	0	[illegible] L.C.O.	
1	0	39	3	5	0	6	7	0	4	15	0	5	15	0	69 L.C.O.	
3	0	[illegible]	7	15	0	14	9	0	10	15	0	7	10	0	[illegible] L.C.O.	
8	0	[illegible]	6	15	0	13	10	10	9	10	0	7	10	0	63 L.C.O.	
7	2	8	14	10	0	[illegible]	4	0	[illegible]	0	0	16	0	0	[illegible] L.C.O.	
3	1	17	3	5	0	7	16	0	5	15	0	4	15	0	4 L.C.O.	
4	3	17	15	10	0	19	15	5	14	7	0	10	14	0	66 L.C.O.	
8	3	[illegible]	7	10	0	18	10	0	11	10	0	9	10	0	71 L.C.O.	
1	1	19	3	5	6	6	5	2	5	0	0	3	6	0	46 L.C.O.	
22	1	5	23	0	0	41	10	0	[illegible]	0	0	28	0	0	186 L.C.O.	
3	0	36	4	10	0	6	3	0	4	15	0	3	15	0	181 L.C.O.	
[illegible]	3	39	124	10	0	[illegible]	9	5	175	4	0	131	17	0		

II.

RETURN

ACCORDING TO PROVINCES AND COUNTIES

OF

JUDICIAL RENTS

FIXED BY

SUB-COMMISSIONS AND CIVIL BILL COURTS,

FOR FIRST AND SECOND STATUTORY TERMS

THAT HAVE BEEN REVISED BY THE LAND COMMISSION

ON APPEAL,

AS NOTIFIED DURING THE MONTH OF

APRIL, 1897.

INDEX.

FIRST STATUTORY TERM.

SUMMARY FOR APRIL, 1897.

Number of Cases in which Judicial Rents have been fixed after Rehearing.	Province and County.	Extent of Holding, Statute.			Poor Law Valuation.			Former Rent.			Judicial Rent.			Rent Fixed on Appeal.		
	ULSTER—	A.	R.	P.	£	s.	d.	£	s.	d.	£	s.	d.	£	s.	d.
4	Armagh, ...	23	0	0	27	10	0	25	8	7	15	17	8	17	13	6
1	Cavan, ...	19	1	6	17	10	0	23	3	5	19	0	0	19	16	0
5	Donegal, ...	222	3	37	63	15	0	83	6	11	66	5	0	62	10	0
1	Tyrone, ...	9	0	8	8	15	0	7	18	8	6	15	0	6	15	0
Total, 11		284	1	4	117	10	0	149	11	8	108	17	6	103	11	6
	LEINSTER—															
6	Wexford, ...	255	0	24	173	15	0	204	17	6	148	18	0	149	15	0
Total, 6		255	0	24	173	15	0	204	17	6	148	15	0	149	15	0
	MUNSTER—															
1	Cork, ...	28	0	23	21	10	0	27	0	0	21	15	6	23	10	0
1	Kerry, ...	121	3	11	14	15	0	26	0	0	20	10	0	20	0	0
Total, 2		149	3	34	36	5	0	53	0	0	42	5	6	43	10	0

IRELAND.

FIRST STATUTORY TERM

PROVINCE OF

COUNTY OF

Appeal No.	Record Register.	Date of Order.	Name of Tenant.	Name of Landlord.	Poor Law Union.	Townland.
		1897.				
2155	10981	March 27,	Terence O'Hare, ...	Countess of Charlemont	Armagh, ...	Drumerten, ...
2156	10997	"	Daniel Rafferty, ...	do.	do. ...	Cladymore, ...
2160	11014	"	Arthur M'Keown, ...	Jane Hilton, ...	do. ...	Tamlat. ...
2162	11017	"	Thomas Callan, ...	Count de Salis, ...	Banbridge, ...	Ballyfrenk, ...
2161		March 24,	Do.	do.	do. ...	do. ...
						Total, ...

COUNTY OF

Appeal No.	Record Register.	Date of Order.	Name of Tenant.	Name of Landlord.	Poor Law Union.	Townland.
1411	7859	Feb. 24,	Robert Jameson, ...	Baroness Liegar (Exors. of)	Bailieborough, ...	Kilmurvan, ...
						Total, ...

COUNTY OF

Appeal No.	Record Register.	Date of Order.	Name of Tenant.	Name of Landlord.	Poor Law Union.	Townland.
2540	12515	March 6,	William Mathews, ...	Elizabeth Riky, ...	Strabane, ...	Cavanyellan, ...
2539		"	Do.	do.	do. ...	do. ...
2549	12546	"	William M'Garvey, ...	William M'Kay, ...	Milford, ...	Crowshall, ...
2548	12551	March 12,	Michael M'Fadden, ...	Aaron Wilson, ...	do. ...	Couart, ...
2541	12524	"	Robert Armstrong, ...	Sir T. H. Hayes, Bart., ...	Stranorlar, ...	Creggan, ...
2543	12517	"	H. Sweeney (Admor. of),	Col. R. G. Montgomery, ...	do. ...	Trentaboy, ...
						Total, ...

ULSTER.

ARMAGH.

Appellant.	Extent of Holding			Poor Law Valuation.			Former Rent.			Judicial Rent.			Rent fixed on Appeal.			Observations.
	A.	R.	P.	£	s.	d.	£	s.	d.	£	s.	d.	£	s.	d.	
L.	4	0	29	6	0	0	5	4	0	8	16	0	3	15	0	
L.	11	8	17	7	5	0	6	6	0	3	5	0	4	0	0	
L.	13	2	34	21	10	0	10	16	7	7	17	6	7	17	6	
T. } L. }	3	1	30	2	15	0	3	14	0	2	0	0	2	0	0	
	33	0	0	37	10	0	26	2	7	16	17	6	17	12	6	

CAVAN.

Appellant.	A.	R.	P.	£	s.	d.	£	s.	d.	£	s.	d.	£	s.	d.	Observations.
L.	19	1	5	17	10	0	22	3	6	19	0	0	19	14	0	
	19	1	5	17	10	0	22	3	6	19	0	0	19	14	0	

DONEGAL.

Appellant.	A.	R.	P.	£	s.	d.	£	s.	d.	£	s.	d.	£	s.	d.	Observations.
L. } T. }	31	0	30	22	10	0	25	0	0	18	0	0	16	5	0	
L.	61	1	0	24	5	0	30	5	5	20	0	0	20	0	0	
L.	7	3	20	—			3	0	0	2	0	0	2	0	0	
L.	107	2	16	19	10	0	28	10	8	21	0	0	11	0	0	
L.	31	3	5	7	10	0	7	10	0	4	5	0	4	5	0	
	272	3	31	83	15	0	96	5	11	66	5	0	53	10	0	

PROVINCE OF

COUNTY OF

Appeal No.	Record Number.	Date of Order.	Name of Tenant.	Name of Landlord.	Poor Law Union.	Townland.
		1887.				
740	[illegible]	19 March.	Patrick Corrigan, ...	Sir John Talbot Power, Bart.	Enniscorthy, ...	Ballyvaldon, ...
745	[illegible]	"	Michael Dunnion, ...	do.	do., ...	do. ...
741	[illegible]	18 March.	William Murphy, ...	Mrs. A. Bettys & another,	Wexford, ...	Grange, ...
725	[illegible]	"	J. Quigley & another,	James Hawkins, ...	do., ...	[illegible] ...
187	[illegible]	"	Richard Murdoch, ...	The Misses Bayley, ..	do., ...	Kilbeg, ...
186	[illegible]	"	Patrick [illegible], ...	James Boyd, ...	do., ...	Ballyboro, ...
						Total, ...

PROVINCE OF

COUNTY OF

Appeal No.	Record Number.	Date of Order.	Name of Tenant.	Name of Landlord.	Poor Law Union.	Townland.
3434	13643	21 April,	Thomas Connell, ...	Lord Carbery, ...	Skibbereen, ...	The Caherus, ...
3431		"	Do., ...	do., ...	do., ...	do., ...
						Total, ...

COUNTY OF

Appeal No.	Record Number.	Date of Order.	Name of Tenant.	Name of Landlord.	Poor Law Union.	Townland.
2278	7896	26 Jan.	Timothy Lynch, ...	P. O. Mayberry & anor., ...	Kenmare, ...	[illegible], ...
2275		"	Do., ...	do., ...	do., ...	do., ...
						Total, ...

FIRST STATUTORY TERM.

LEINSTER.

WEXFORD.

Appellant.	Extent of Holding. Statute.			Poor Law Valuation.			Former Rent.			Judicial Rent.			Rent fixed on Appeal.			Observations.
	A.	R.	P.	£	s.	d.	£	s.	d.	£	s.	d.	£	s.	d.	
L.	80	0	0	25	0	0	28	7	2	18	0	0	19	5	0	
L.	47	3	35	22	0	0	34	0	10	18	0	0	18	0	0	
L.	4	1	16	5	10	0	7	18	3	4	5	0	6	0	0	
L.	40	3	32	25	0	0	33	10	0	20	10	0	24	0	0	
T.	44	2	8	64	0	0	74	1	4	60	0	0	58	10	0	
T.	43	2	22	32	0	0	37	0	0	28	0	0	30	0	0	
	260	0	24	173	10	0	204	17	5	168	15	0	169	15	0	

MUNSTER.

CORK.

Appellant.	A.	R.	P.	£	s.	d.	£	s.	d.	£	s.	d.	£	s.	d.	Observations.
T. / L.	36	0	23	81	10	0	97	0	0	51	16	6	83	10	0	
	36	0	23	81	10	0	37	0	0	51	16	6	83	10	0	

KERRY.

Appellant.	A.	R.	P.	£	s.	d.	£	s.	d.	£	s.	d.	£	s.	d.	Observations.
T. / L.	111	3	11	16	15	0	26	0	0	20	10	0	20	0	0	
	111	3	11	16	15	0	26	0	0	20	10	0	20	0	0	

CIVIL BILLS.

FIRST STATUTORY TERM.

SUMMARY FOR APRIL, 1897.

Number of Cases in which Judicial Rents have been fixed.	Province and County.	Extent of Holdings, Statute.	Poor Law Valuation.	Former Rent.	Judicial Rent.	Rent fixed on Appeal.
	ULSTER—	A. R. P.	£ s. d.	£ s. d.	£ s. d.	£ s. d.
1	Cavan, ...	57 3 10	16 15 0	12 0 0	9 15 0	11 10 0
	Total, ...	57 3 10	16 15 0	12 0 0	9 15 0	11 10 0
	MUNSTER—					
2	Kerry, ...	107 1 8	77 10 0	146 0 0	90 16 0	90 16 0
	Total, ...	107 1 8	77 10 0	146 0 0	90 16 0	90 16 0

IRELAND.

1	ULSTER, ...	57 3 10	16 15 0	12 0 0	9 15 0	11 10 0
2	MUNSTER, ...	107 1 8	77 10 0	146 0 0	90 16 0	90 16 0
TOTAL, 3		165 0 18	94 5 0	158 0 0	100 11 0	102 6 0

FIRST STATUTORY TERM.

CIVIL BILL

PROVINCE OF

COUNTY OF

Appeal No.	Report Number	Date of Order	Name of Tenant	Name of Landlord	Poor Law Union	Townland
		1896.				
1409	1646 C.R.	Dec. 12.	Mary J. Flanagan, ..	J. B. Singleton, ..	Bailieborough, ..	Kilnacrandy, ..
						Total, ..

PROVINCE OF

COUNTY OF

COURTS.

ULSTER.

CAVAN.

Appellant.	Extent of Holding, Statute.	Poor Law Valuation.	Former Rent.	Judicial Rent.	Rent fixed on Appeal.	Observations.
	A. R. P.	£ s. d.	£ s. d.	£ s. d.	£ s. d.	
L.	87 3 16	18 16 0	13 0 0	9 15 0	11 10 0	
	87 3 16	18 16 0	13 0 0	9 15 0	11 10 0	

SUMMARY FOR APRIL, 1897.

SECOND STATUTORY TERM.

Province and County.	Number of Cases in which Judicial Rents have been fixed.	Acreage of Holding. Statute			Poor Law Valuation.			Rent of Holding prior to creation of First Statutory Term.			Judicial Rent for First Statutory Term.			Judicial Rent for Second Statutory Term.			Rent fixed on Appeal.		
		A.	R.	P.	£	s.	d.	£	s.	d.	£	s.	d.	£	s.	d.	£	s.	d.
ULSTER—																			
Armagh, ...	21	403	[illegible]	15	458	0	0	535	14	5	405	0	0	363	18	4	775	18	0
Donegal, ...	1	79	1	0	7	0	0	18	0	0	10	16	0	10	15	0	10	15	0
Down, ...	1	18	0	8	18	10	0	19	0	0	17	0	0	13	5	0	14	10	8
Londonderry, ...	9	470	2	38	415	10	0	467	13	8	326	11	8	237	14	6	253	13	4
Tyrone, ...	3	64	3	35	54	5	0	58	8	3	46	15	0	35	5	0	35	8	0
Total, ...	34	1,035	3	17	959	5	0	1,071	9	10	806	1	8	560	0	0	[illegible]	13	6
MUNSTER—																			
Cork, ...	1	50	2	3	21	5	0	45	0	0	33	15	0	34	0	0	[illegible]	10	0
Total, ...	1	50	2	3	21	5	0	45	0	0	33	15	0	34	0	0	[illegible]	10	0

IRELAND.

SECOND STATUTORY TERM.

PROVINCE OF

COUNTY OF

Appeal Number.	Record Number.	Date of Order.	Name of Tenant.	Name of Landlord.	Poor Law Union.	Townland.
		1897.				
4	49	March 19,	Thomas Cunningham,	John G. Cape, ...	Armagh, ...	[illegible], ...
76	86	„ 17,	Wm. Flanagan, ...	Wm. Bryans, ...	do., ...	Dunavan, ...
73	205	„ 24,	Joseph Stevenson, ...	Rev. W. J. Leslie, ...	Banbridge, ...	Moyarlaw, ...
74	225	„ „	James Porter, ...	do. do. ...	do., ...	do., ...
79	170	„ 27,	Michael M'Closkey, ...	J. H. B. Todd Thornton,	Armagh, ...	Ballyquin[illegible]
73	150	„ „	Wm. Dinsmore, ...	James Dunlop, ...	do., ...	Ballymurry, ...
77	36	„ 24,	John Knipe, ...	Lt.-Col. P. Tarris and another,	do., ...	Artasooly, ...
75	96	„ „	John Best, ...	Capt. R. Small, ...	Newry, ...	Mullaglass, ...
33	79	„ 27,	James Craig, ...	Wm. Robinson (Reps. of),	Armagh, ...	Cranagh, ...
62	76	„ „	Daniel Campbell, ...	do. do. ...	do., ...	Knockrevan, ...
61	77	„ „	Alex. M'Cartan, ...	Jane Dunlop and others,	do., ...	Moville, ...
58	63	„ „	Ed. M'Geown, ...	do. do. ...	do., ...	Tullybrannigan,
66	78	„ „	Patk. M'Veery, ...	do. do. ...	do., ...	Moville, ...
59a	60	„ 24,	Patk. M'Kernan, ...	[illegible] Hy. Burgess, ...	do., ...	Ballymacdo, ...
110	642	„ „	Hugh Hazzard, ...	J. R. Stanley (Trus. of),	Lurgan, ...	Derrykeevan, ...
103		„ „	Do., ...	do. do. ...	do., ...	do., ...
117	641	„ „	Maria Hall, ...	do. do. ...	do., ...	do., ...
102		„ „	Do., ...	do. do. ...	do., ...	do., ...
104	656	„ „	James Strain, ...	do. do. ...	do., ...	do., ...
119		„ „	Do., ...	do. do. ...	do., ...	do., ...
49	164	„ „	Thomas Collins,	Count de Salis, ...	Banbridge, ...	Ballykeel, ...
43		„ „	Do., ...	do. do. ...	do., ...	do., ...
61	123	„ „	Do., ...	do. do. ...	do., ...	Ballyfish, ...
60		„ „	Do., ...	do. do. ...	do., ...	do., ...
63	159	„ „	Alexander Watson, ...	do. do. ...	do., ...	Corcreevy and T[illegible],
61		„ „	Do., ...	do. do. ...	do., ...	do., ...
64	73	„ 27,	Robert Allen, ...	R. J. M'Geough, ...	Armagh, ...	Legaghory, ...
						Total, ...

ULSTER.

ARMAGH.

Applicant.	Extent of Holding Statute.	Poor Law Valuation.	Rent of Holding prior to fixing of First Statutory Term.	Judicial Rent for First Statutory Term.	Judicial Rent for Second Statutory Term.	Rent Fixed on Appeal.	Observations.
	A. R. P.	£ s. d.	£ s. d.	£ s. d.	£ s. d.	£ s. d.	
L.	7 2 0	6 10 0	9 1 10	6 0 0	7 12 6	5 5 0	
L.	21 0 0	30 0 0	[illegible] 0 0	21 0 0	21 8 6	12 2 6	
L.	17 0 0	16 15 0	22 1 3	15 10 0	11 0 0	11 0 0	
L.	20 0 14	19 15 0	23 5 0	16 10 0	12 15 0	14 10 0	
L.	20 1 20	23 0 0	37 11 10	23 10 0	13 13 0	13 13 0	
L.	5 0 0	9 0 0	9 17 6	8 0 0	5 0 0	6 0 0	
L.	45 2 35	38 0 0	83 11 9	60 0 0	37 0 0	28 0 0	
L.	31 3 [illegible]	77 0 0	96 3 0	31 0 0	13 5 0	15 5 0	
L.	10 0 36	5 5 0	11 9 8	6 10 0	4 17 0	5 17 0	
L.	11 1 5	10 10 0	13 1 0	6 0 0	6 5 0	6 16 0	
L.	19 2 20	18 15 0	19 17 3	16 0 0	9 9 6	10 10 0	
L.	14 2 5	15 5 0	20 0 0	15 0 0	10 0 0	10 0 0	
L.	7 0 0	4 5 0	6 15 0	7 0 0	4 1 6	4 1 6	
L.	12 1 0	15 10 0	15 10 0	11 10 0	9 0 0	9 0 0	
T. L.	12 2 0	15 0 0	18 15 0	12 10 0	8 18 0	8 15 0	
T. L.	9 0 0	9 5 0	12 7 6	7 10 0	5 5 0	5 5 0	
L. T.	9 0 0	5 15 0	11 15 0	6 0 0	4 0 0	4 0 0	
T. L.	30 0 0	44 0 0	64 15 8	35 0 0	21 0 0	23 15 0	
L. T.	15 2 36	23 10 0	29 3 6	21 10 0	14 18 0	15 12 0	
T. L.	73 3 30	87 5 0	88 19 2	74 0 0	60 0 0	60 0 0	
T.	14 3 0	18 18 0	12 11 0	10 0 0	9 5 0	9 5 0	
	401 2 15	463 0 0	563 14 5	408 0 0	288 18 6	278 10 0	

SECOND STATUTORY TERM.

COUNTY OF

Appeal No.	Record Number.	Date of Order.	Name of Tenant.	Name of Landlord.	Poor Law Union.	Townland.
1	1	1897. March 6,	James Kee, —	W. Young (Trus. of), —	Stranorlar, —	Convoy, —
						Total, —

COUNTY OF

Appeal No.	Record Number.	Date of Order.	Name of Tenant.	Name of Landlord.	Poor Law Union.	Townland.
189?	147	March 24,	John O'Hare, —	[illegible], E. Corry, —	Newry, —	[illegible] —
						Total, —

COUNTY OF

Appeal No.	Record Number.	Date of Order.	Name of Tenant.	Name of Landlord.	Poor Law Union.	Townland.
7	1	March 6,	Samuel [illegible], —	Lord Templemore, —	Londonderry, —	[illegible], —
8		„	Do., —	do., —	do., —	do., —
5	5	„	John Kane, —	Wm. Rankin, —	Limavady, —	Moneyguiggy, —
6	4	„	William Aitken, —	Archbishop of Armagh,	Londonderry, —	Lettermuck, —
3	8	„	W. J. Cuthbert, —	R. J. C. Young (Trus. of),	do., —	[illegible], —
1		„	Do., — —	do., — —	do., —	do., —
2	7	„	Do., … —	do., — —	do., —	do., —
4		„	Do., — —	do., — —	do., —	do., —
13	6	„	W. J. Watson, —	Robert Jameson Adams,	do., —	[illegible], —
10		„	Do., — —	do., — —	do., —	do., —
11	19	„	Martha Finlay, —	do., — —	do., —	do., —
16		„	Do., — —	do., — —	do., —	do., —
12	20	„	George Watson, —	do., — —	do., —	do., —
9		„	Do., … —	do., — —	do., —	do., —
15	27	„	Michael M'[illegible],	Rev. De la Poer Beresford,	do., —	[illegible], —
						Total, —

COUNTY OF

Appeal No.	Record Number.	Date of Order.	Name of Tenant.	Name of Landlord.	Poor Law Union.	Townland.
4	17	March 5,	J. M'Farland, —	Hon. J. M. Cowper, —	Omagh, —	[illegible], —
5	1	„	Robert Wilson, —	James Evans, —	Dungannon, —	[illegible], —
						Total, —

SECOND STATUTORY TERM.

DONEGAL.

Applicant	Extent of Holding Statute.	Poor Law Valuation	Rent of Holding prior to fixing of First Statutory Term	Judicial Rent for First Statutory Term	Judicial Rent for Second Statutory Term	Rent Fixed on Appeal	Observations
	A. R. P.	£ s. d.	£ s. d.	£ s. d.	£ s. d.	£ s. d.	
T.	78 3 0	7 0 0	18 0 0	10 15 0	10 15 0	10 15 0	
	78 3 0	7 0 0	18 0 0	10 15 0	10 15 0	10 15 0	

DOWN.

Applicant	Extent of Holding Statute.	Poor Law Valuation	Rent of Holding prior to fixing of First Statutory Term	Judicial Rent for First Statutory Term	Judicial Rent for Second Statutory Term	Rent Fixed on Appeal	Observations
L.	13 0 8	18 10 0	18 0 0	17 0 0	12 8 0	14 10 0	
	13 0 8	18 10 0	18 0 0	17 0 0	12 8 0	14 10 0	

LONDONDERRY.

Applicant	Extent of Holding Statute.	Poor Law Valuation	Rent of Holding prior to fixing of First Statutory Term	Judicial Rent for First Statutory Term	Judicial Rent for Second Statutory Term	Rent Fixed on Appeal	Observations
L. T.	80 0 15	64 0 0	63 14 0	34 0 0	36 15 0	40 10 0	
T.	173 1 [illegible]	67 10 0	[illegible] 0 0	35 0 0	[illegible] 10 0	[illegible] 8 0	
T.	6 2 16	3 0 0	5 16 0	6 0 0	4 10 0	3 10 0	
T. L.	104 8 4	108 10 0	132 0 9	[illegible] 0 0	64 0 0	81 10 0	
L. T.	23 0 9	—	34 15 9	19 1 9	13 15 0	15 4 8	
T. L.	56 3 0	64 0 0	61 13 10	48 0 0	[illegible] 10 0	43 14 0	
L.	[illegible] 1 36	18 0 0	23 8 4	16 0 0	13 15 8	15 0 0	

SECOND STATUTORY TERM.

PROVINCE OF

COUNTY OF

Appeal No.	Record Number.	Date of Order.	Name of Tenant.	Name of Landlord.	Poor Law Union.	Townland.
164	1[illegible]7	1877 Mar. 1[illegible],	John J. Cronin, ...	Charles Raycroft, ...	Mountmellick, ...	Kilteale, ...
1[illegible]		"	Do., ...	do., ...	do., ...	do., ...
						Fund ...

CIVIL BILL-

Province and County.	Number of Cases in which Judicial Rents have been fixed.	Extent of Holding. Statute.	Poor Law Valuation.
		A. R. P.	£ s. d.
LEINSTER, (Carlow.) ...	1	[illegible] 0 [illegible]	[illegible] 0 0

CIVIL BILL

PROVINCE OF

MUNSTER.

CORK.

Applicant.	Extent of Holding. Statute.	Poor Law Valuation.	Rent of Holding prior to commencement of First Statutory Term.	Judicial Rent for First Statutory Term.	Judicial Rent for Second Statutory Term.	Rent fixed on Appeal.	Observations.
	A. R. P.	£ s. d.	£ s. d.	£ s. d.	£ s. d.	£ s. d.	
L. } T. }	50 2 3	31 5 0	45 0 0	33 15 0	24 0 0	26 10 0	By consent.
	50 2 3	31 5 0	45 0 0	33 15 0	21 0 0	26 10 0	

IRELAND.

Rent of Holding prior to commencement of First Statutory Term.	Judicial Rent for First Statutory Term.	Judicial Rent for Second Statutory Term.	Rent fixed on Appeal.
£ s. d.	£ s. d.	£ s. d.	£ s. d.
183 17 6	110 0 0	65 0 0	90 0 0

COURTS.

LEINSTER.

CARLOW.

www.ingramcontent.com/pod-product-compliance
Lightning Source LLC
Chambersburg PA
CBHW022145160426
43197CB00009B/1429

* 9 7 8 3 7 4 1 1 9 6 5 2 2 *